COLOR BY NUMBERS
BOOK FOR KIDS AGES 8-12

This Book Belongs To:

_____

_____

Color By Number
For Kids Ages 8-12

Thank you for choosing our coloring book. It's great that you like coloring books as much as we do! These activities offer hours of fun and are a great way to improve your focus and concentration.

There are different themed colorig pages. In this book, we've included various kids of color by number designs for coloring.

Once you complete the book, then you will get a huge collection of unique coloring pages.

Have fun and enjoy!

COLORING TEST PAGE

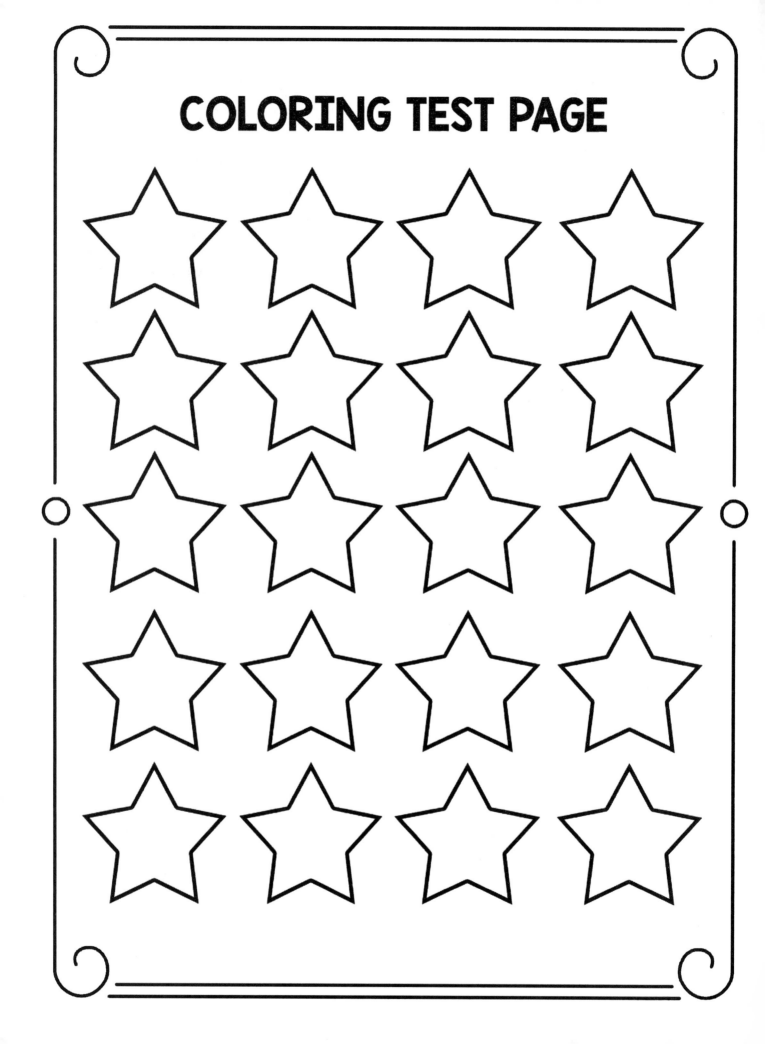

1. Green   2. Olive   3. Rust   4. Red
5. Cyan   6. Yellow

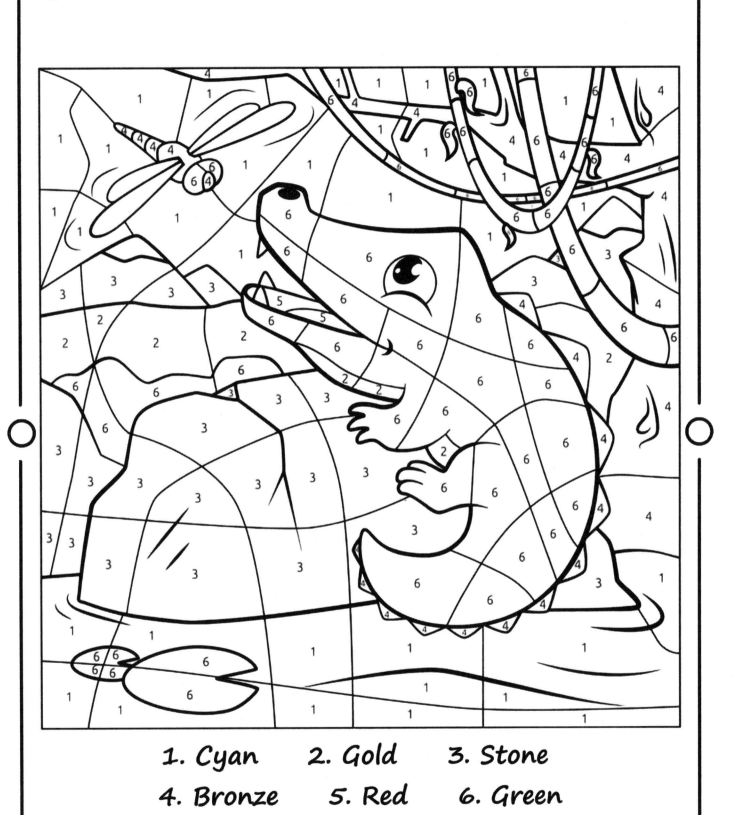

1. Cyan   2. Gold   3. Stone

4. Bronze   5. Red   6. Green

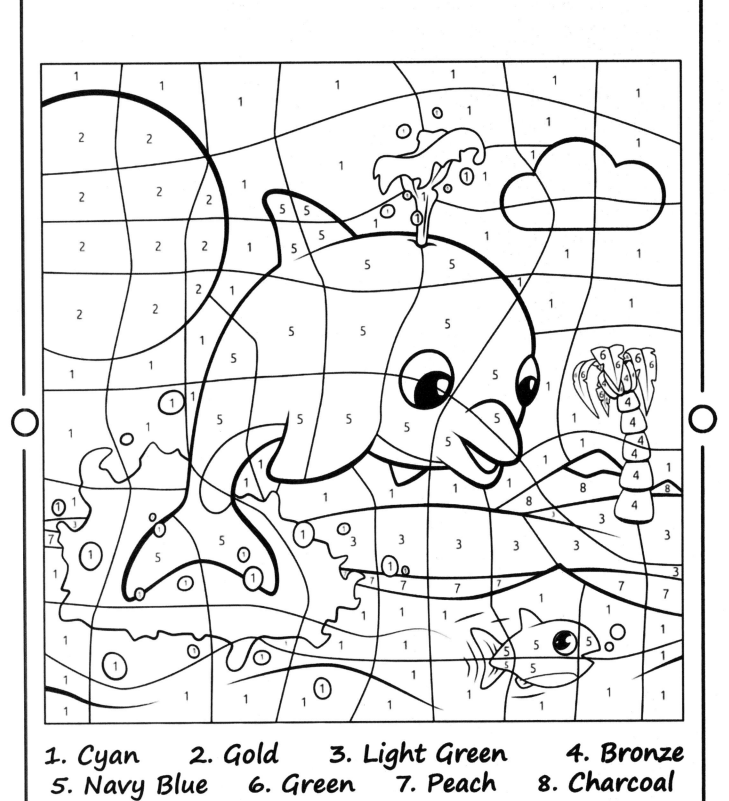

1. Cyan   2. Gold   3. Light Green   4. Bronze
5. Navy Blue   6. Green   7. Peach   8. Charcoal

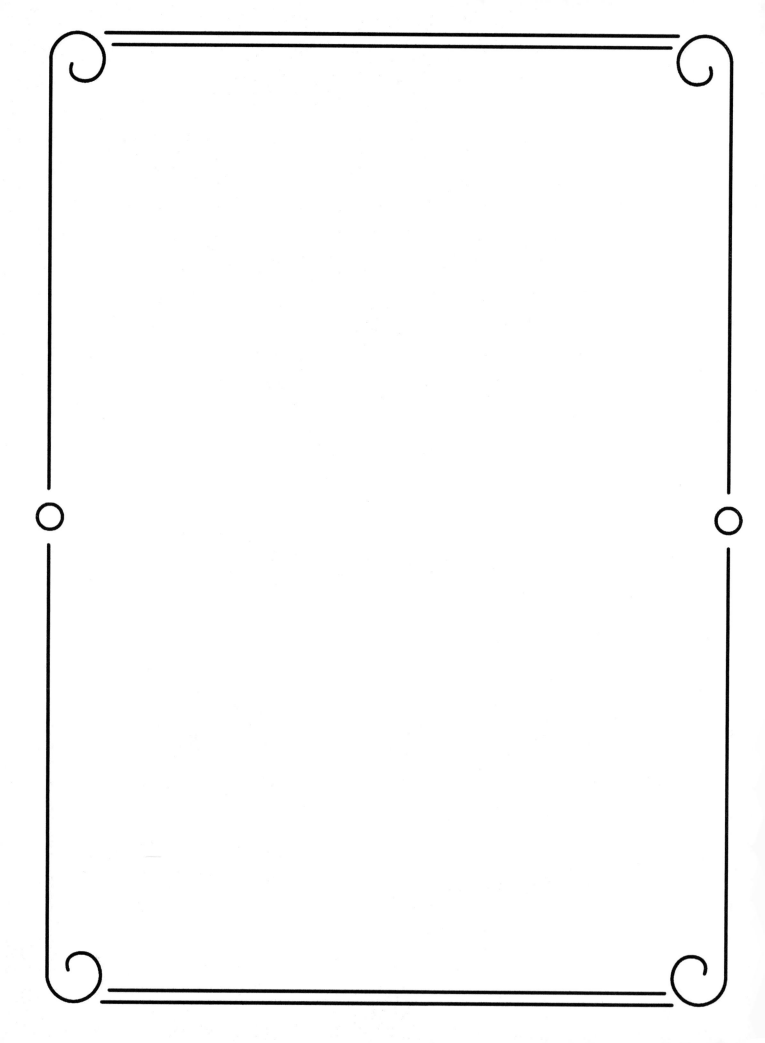

1. Green 2. Orange 3. Maroon 4. Coral
5. Cyan 6. Cream

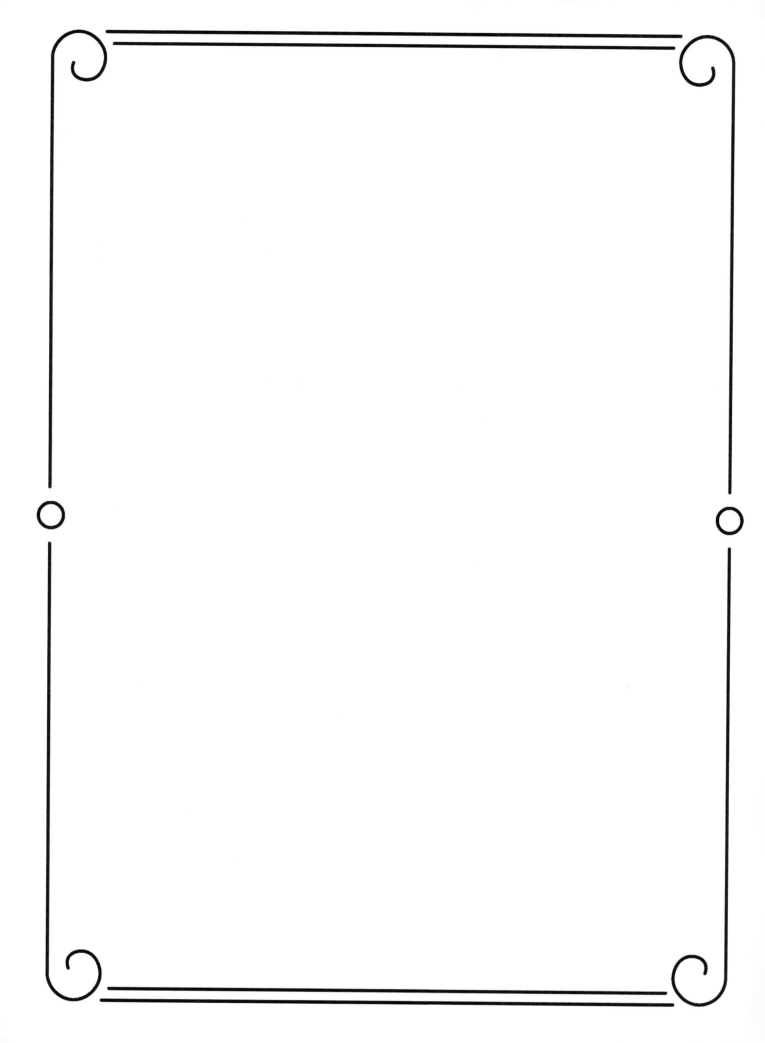

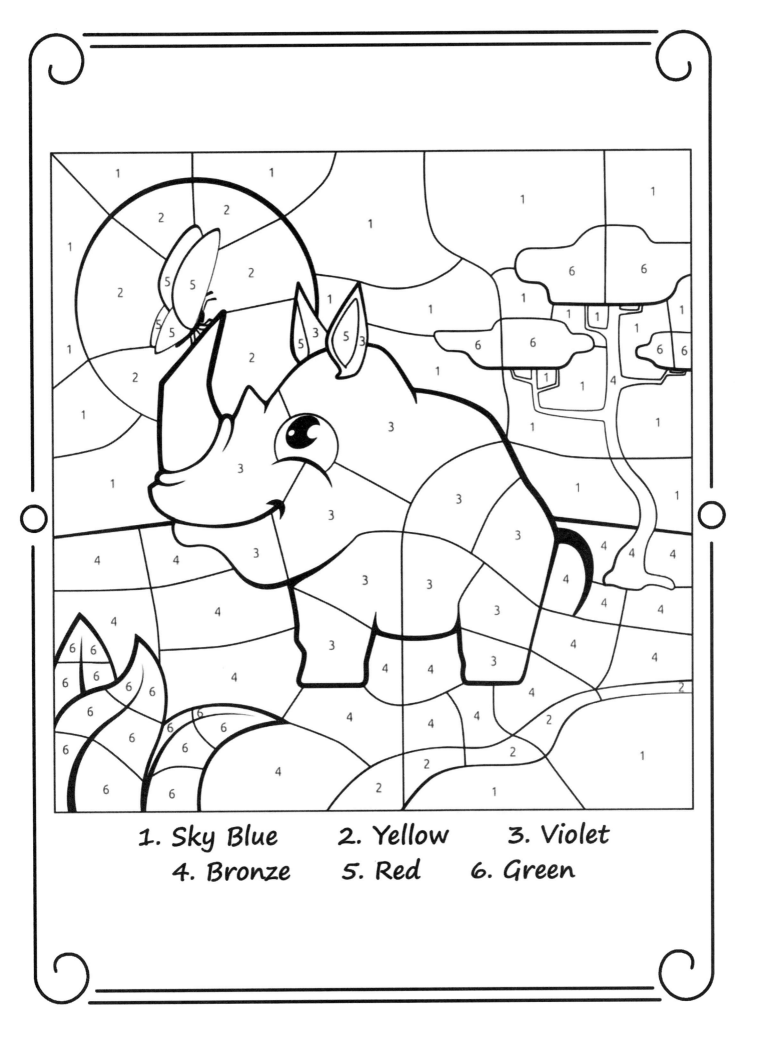

1. Sky Blue   2. Yellow   3. Violet
4. Bronze   5. Red   6. Green

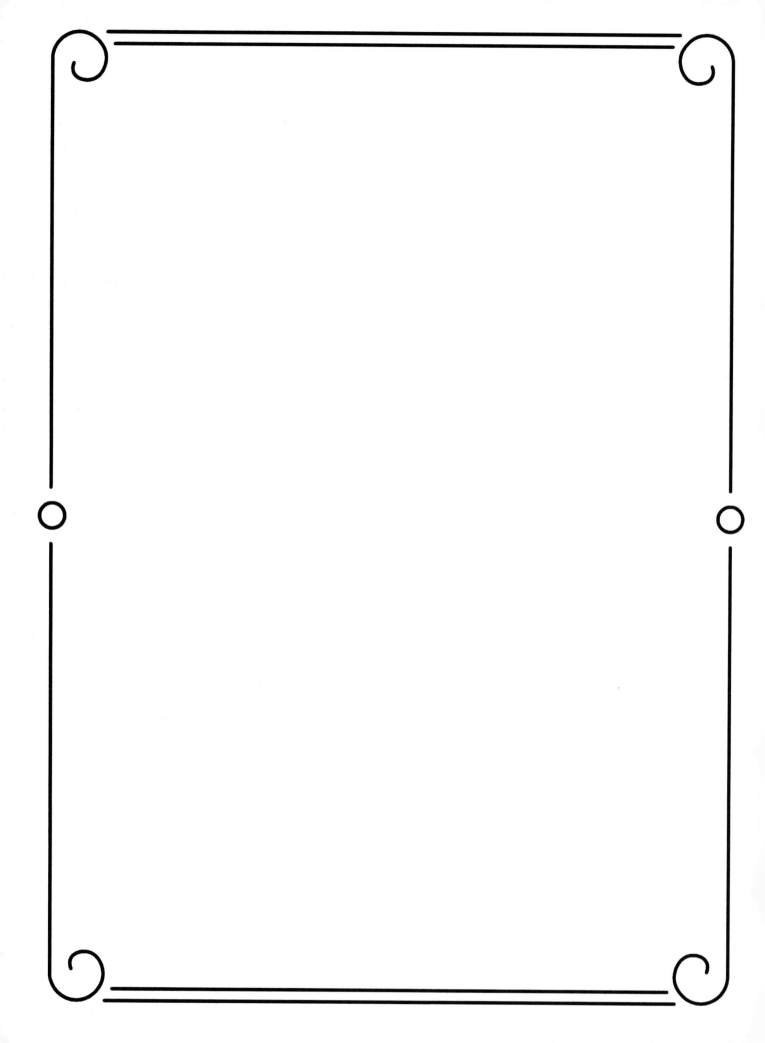

Orange=1   Gray=2 Pink=3 Green=4
Sprinhg Green=5 Aquamarine=6

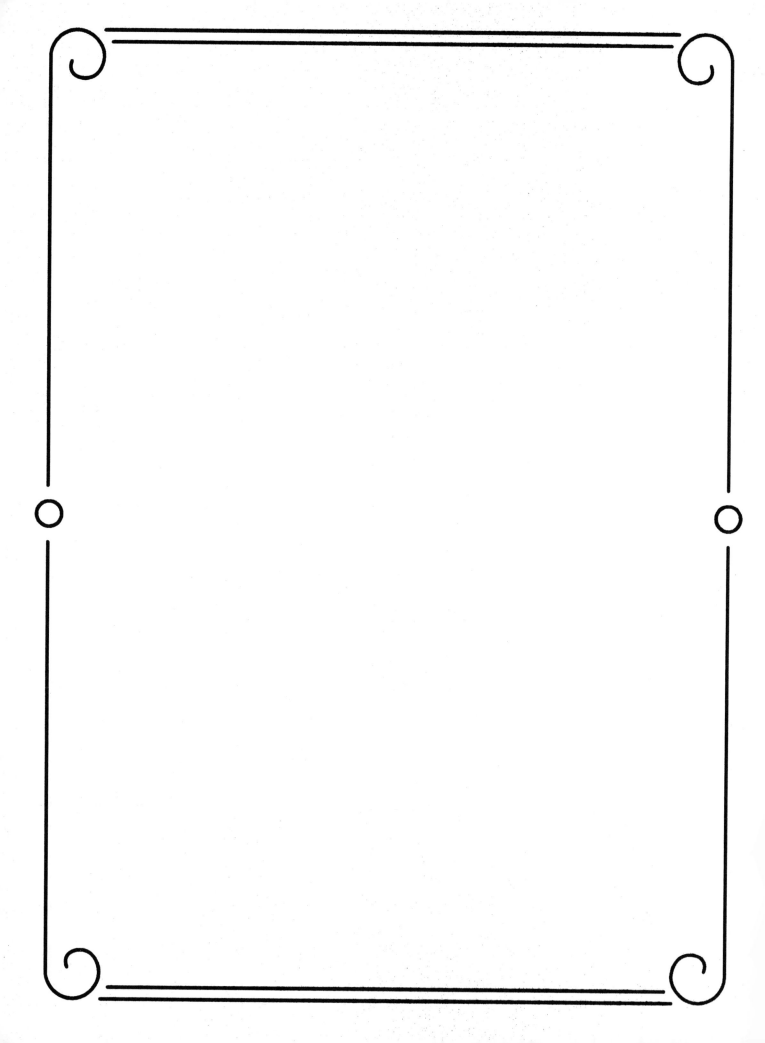

Turquoise=1 Light Cyan=2 Green=3 Yellow=4
Wheat=5 Silver=6 Pink=7 Olive Drab=8

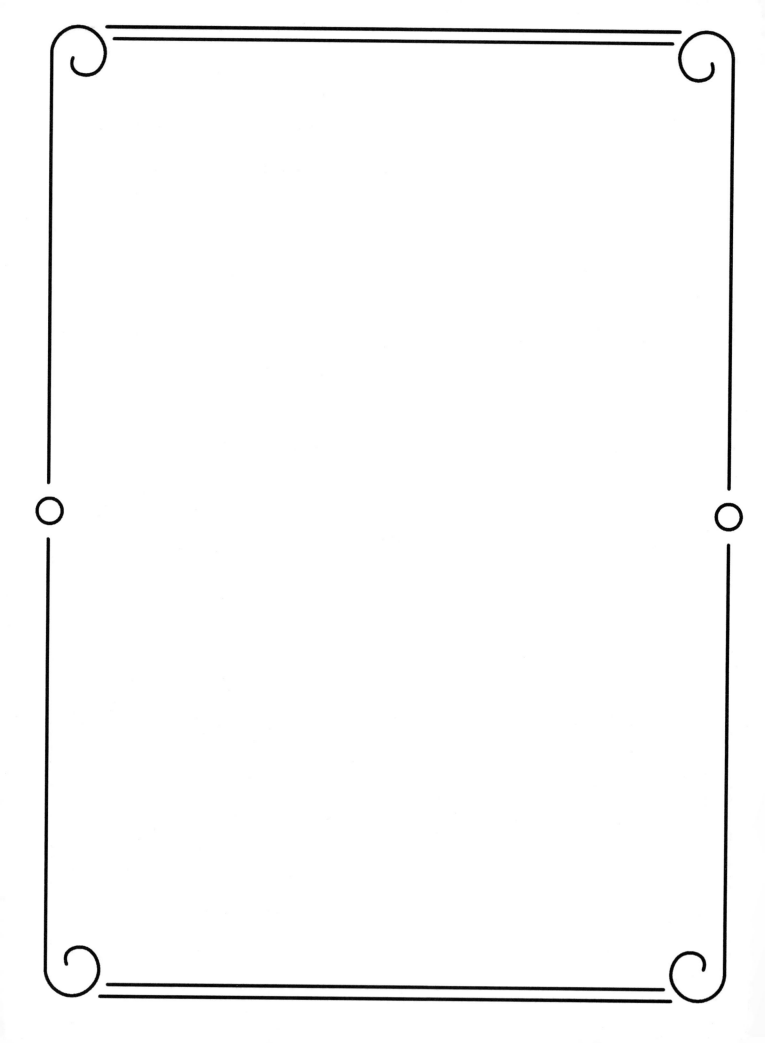

**Yellow=1 Dark Red=2 Gray=3 Dark Blue=4
Pink=5 Olive Drab=6 Aquamarine=7 Light Blue=8**

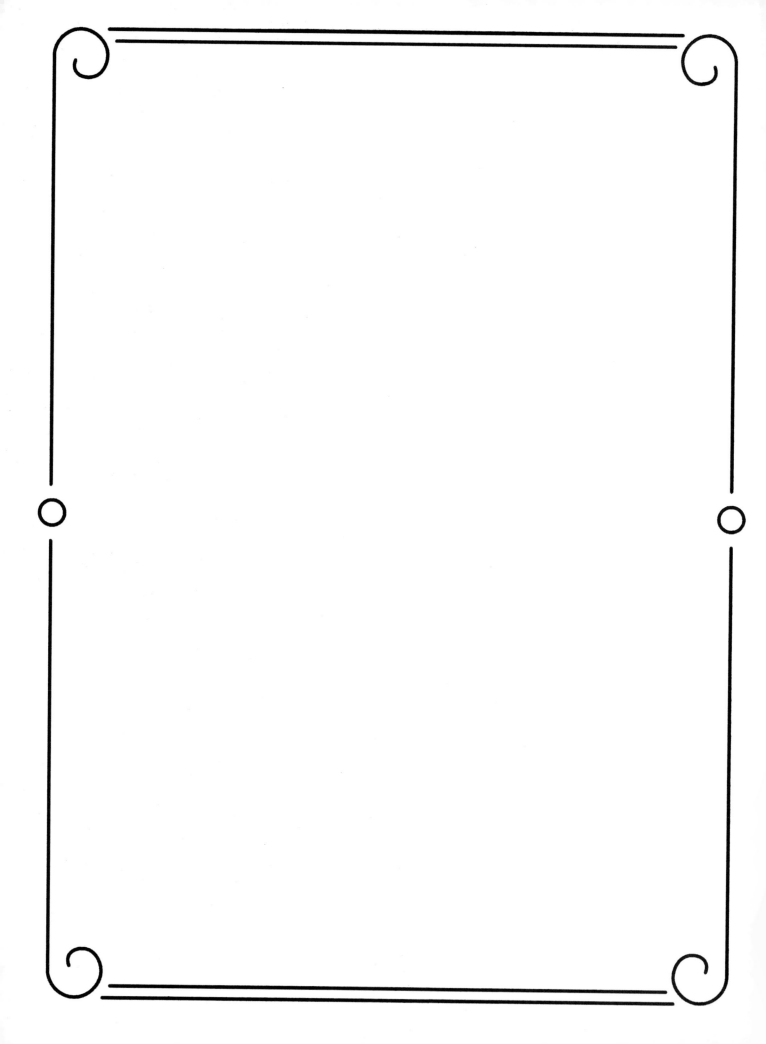

Pink=1   White=2   Red=3   Dark Gray=4
Aquamarine=5   Green=6

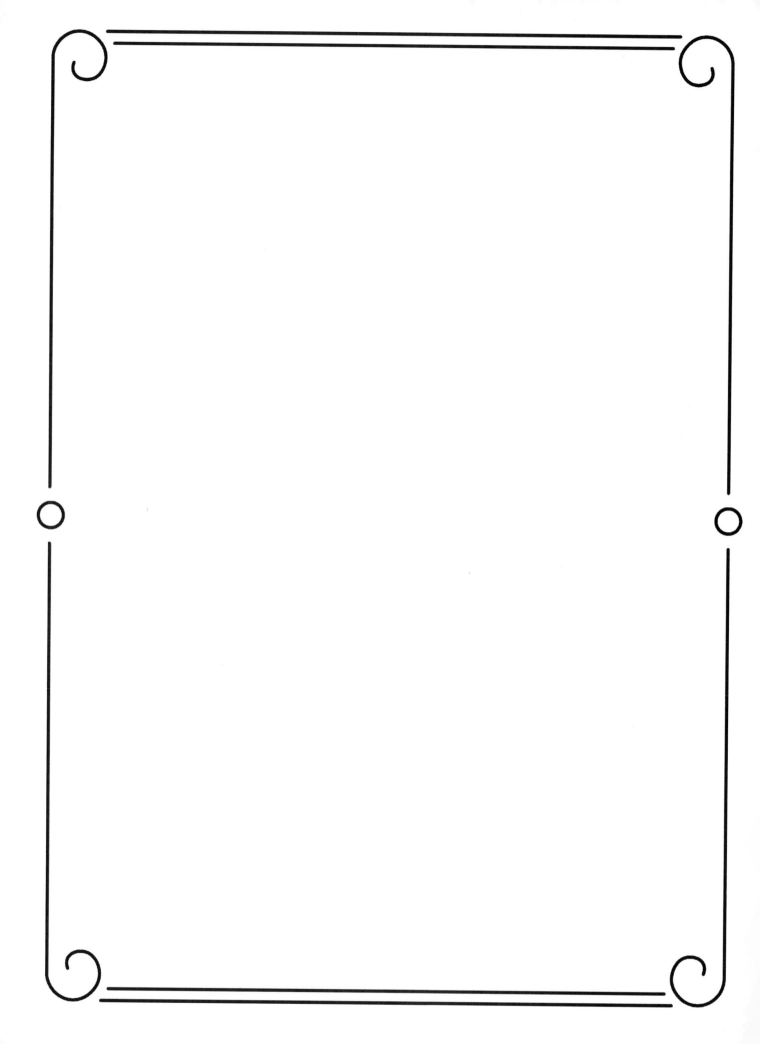

1 - black   2 - light blue   3 - blue   4 - green
5 - yellow   6 - red   7 - orange   8 - violet

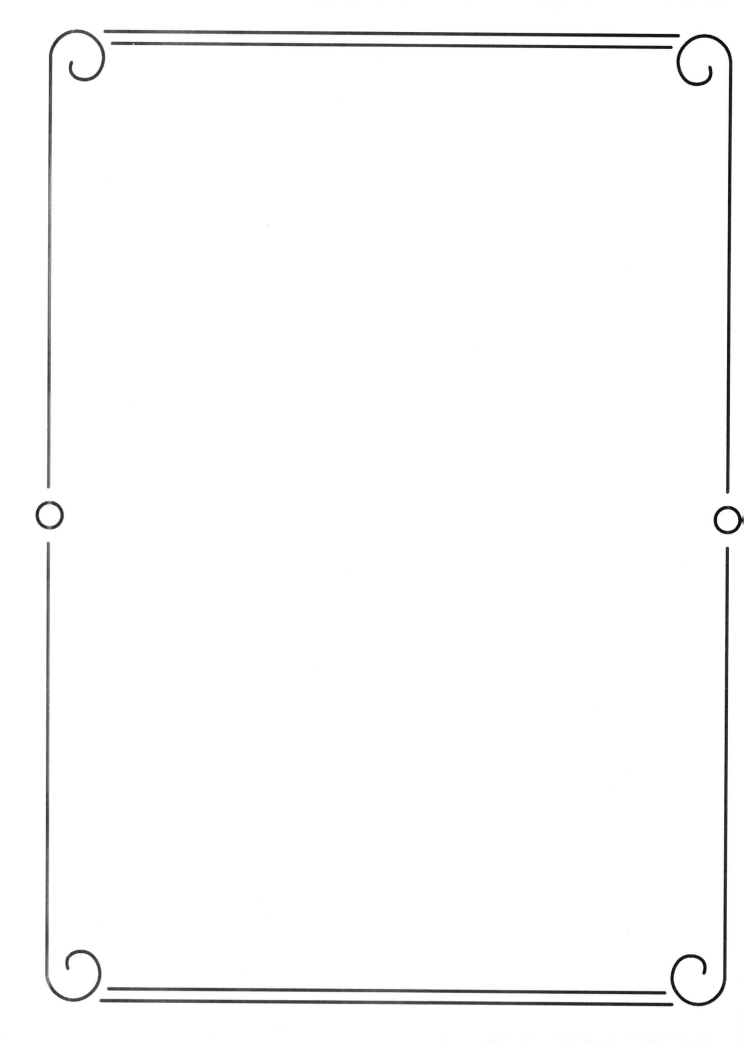

1. Cyan   2. Yellow   3. Light Green
4. Bronze   5. Pink   6. Green

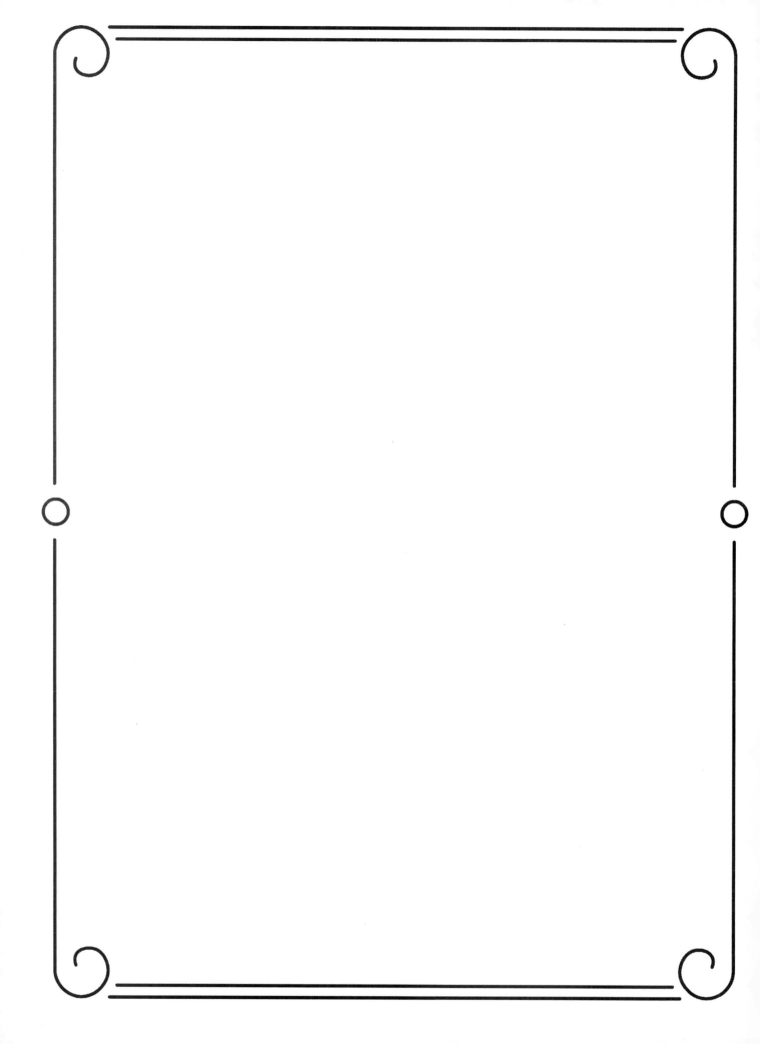

Yellow=1 Red=2 Orange=3 Green=4
Wheat=5 Aquamarine=6

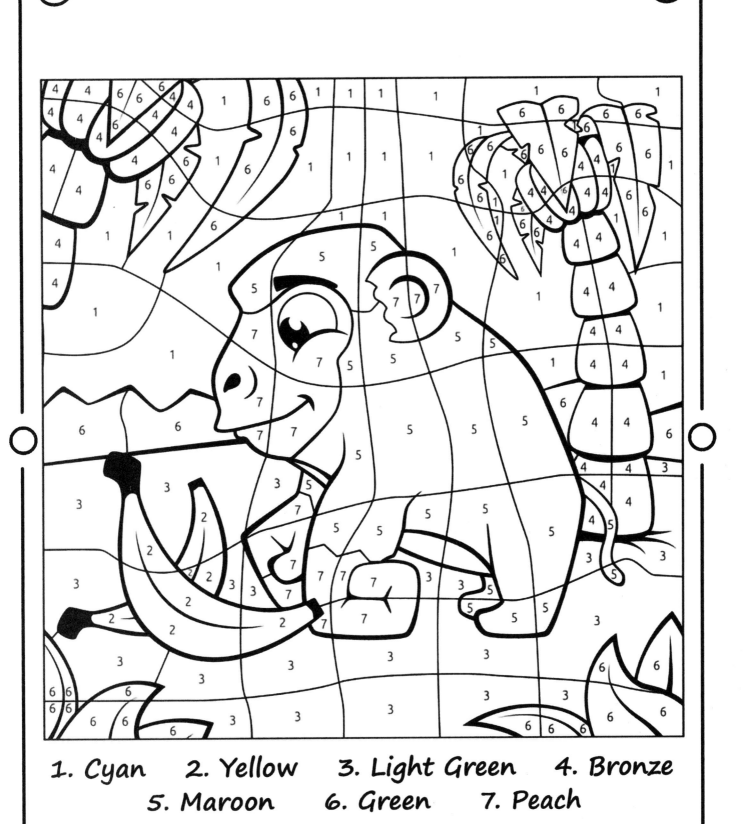

1. Cyan   2. Yellow   3. Light Green   4. Bronze
5. Maroon   6. Green   7. Peach

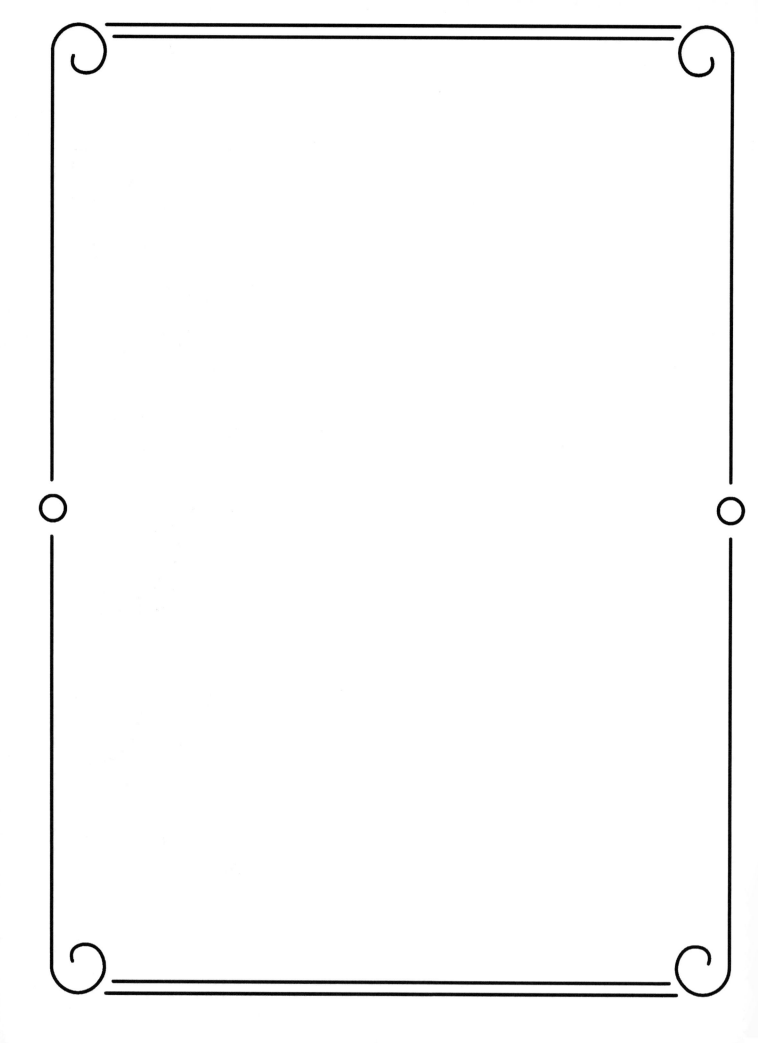

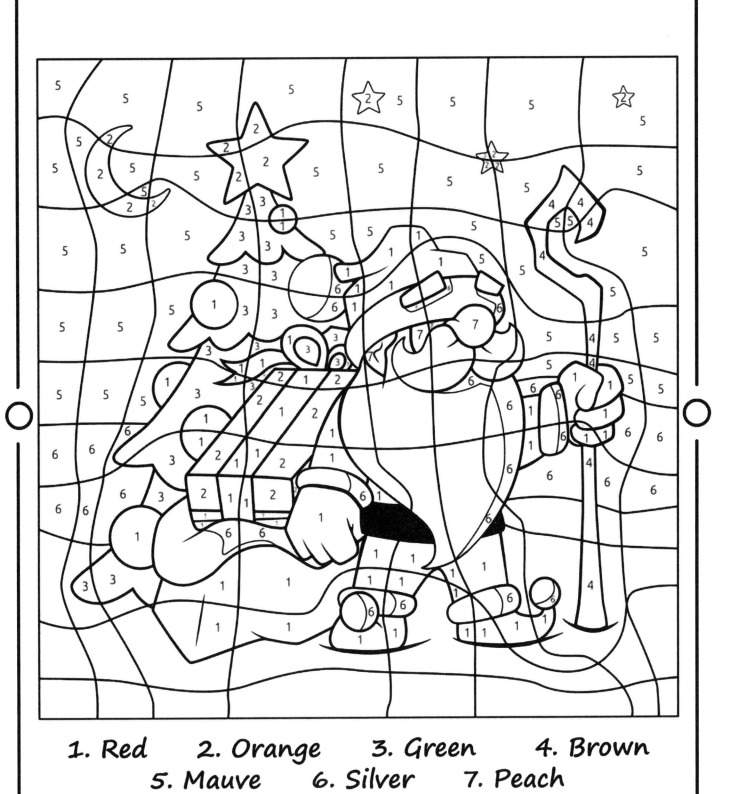

1. Red   2. Orange   3. Green   4. Brown
5. Mauve   6. Silver   7. Peach

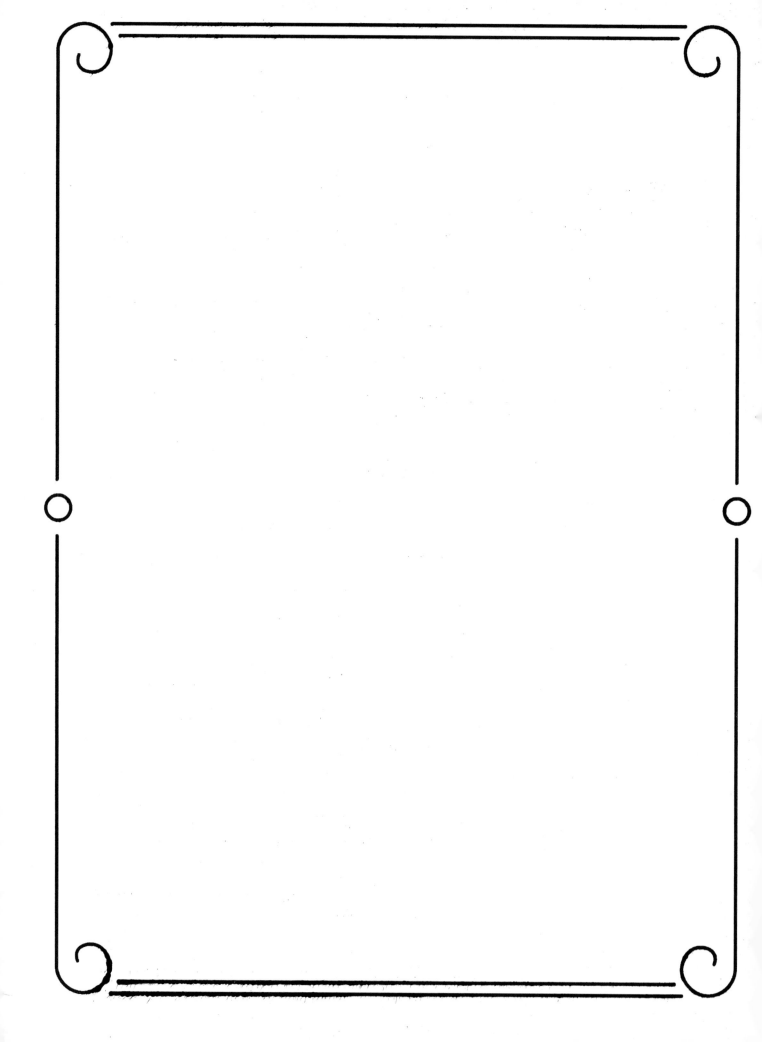

1. Red   2. Cyan   3. Orange   4. Dark Green
5. Green   6. Silver

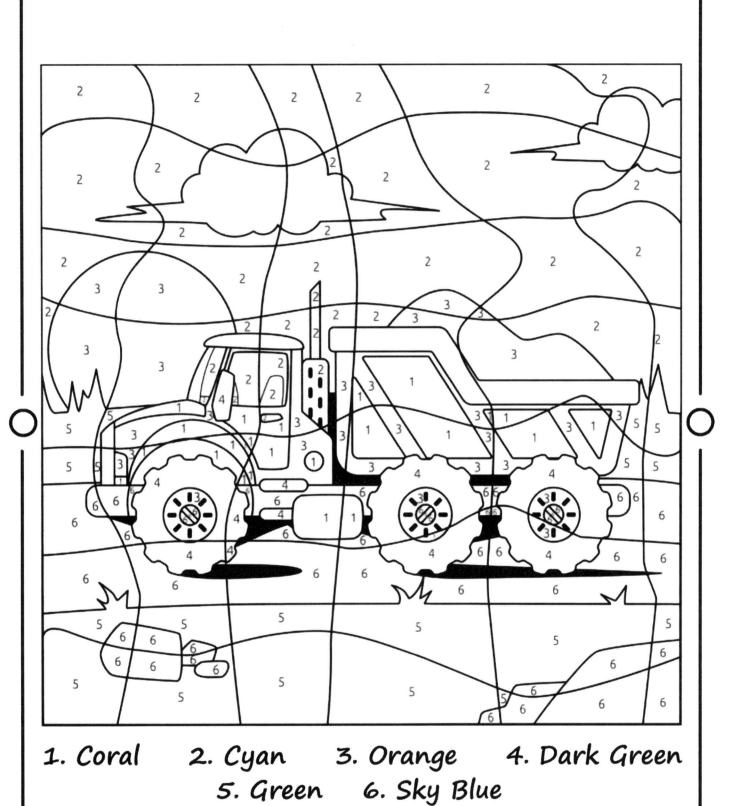

1. Coral   2. Cyan   3. Orange   4. Dark Green
5. Green   6. Sky Blue

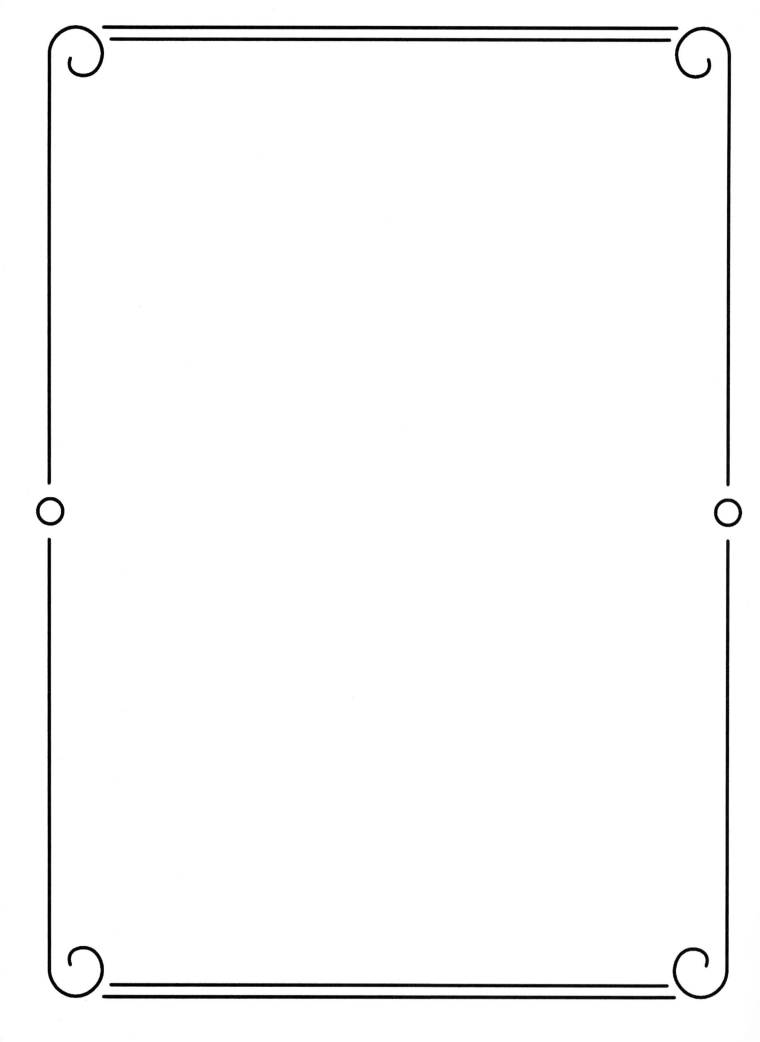

1. Purple   2. Cyan   3. Yellow   4. Dark Green
5. Green   6. Silver   7. Orange   8. Peach

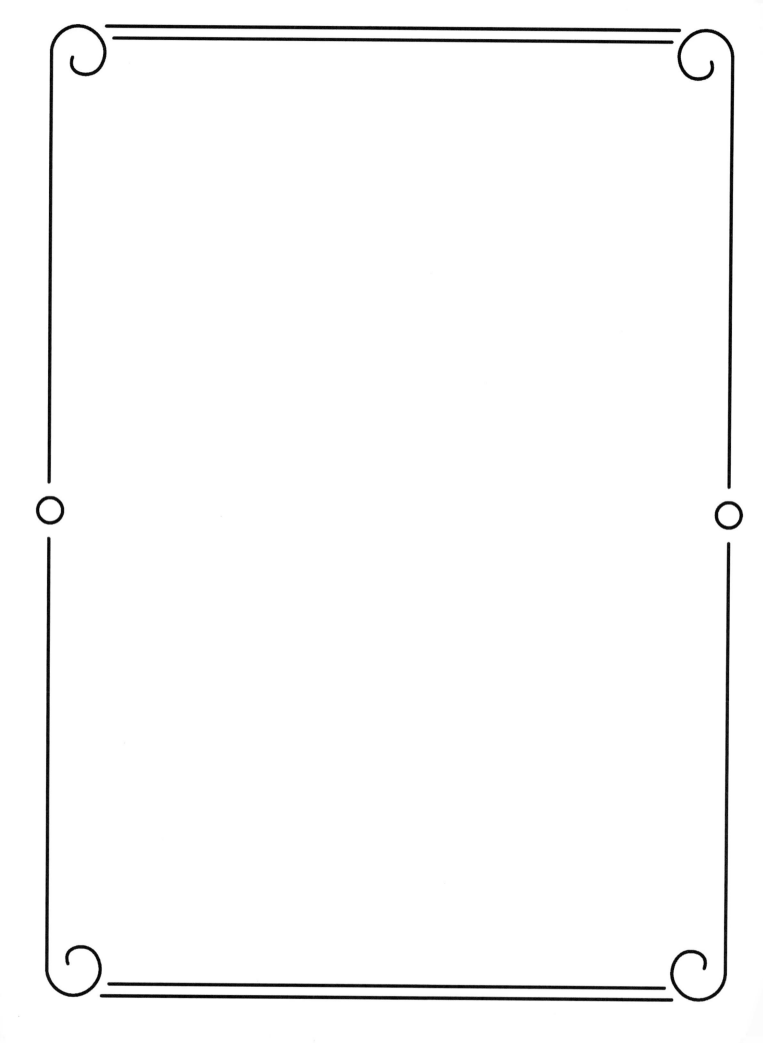

1. Red   2. Cyan   3. Yellow   4. Dark Green
5. Green   6. Lavender   7. Black   8. Maroon

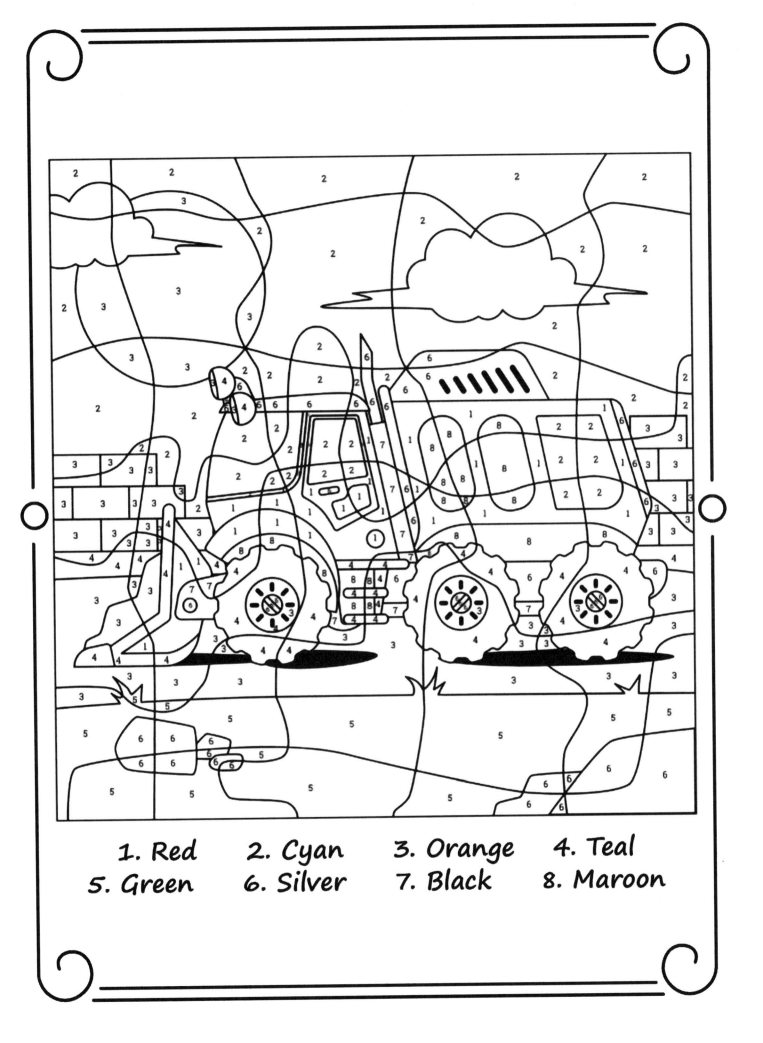

1. Red   2. Cyan   3. Orange   4. Teal
5. Green   6. Silver   7. Black   8. Maroon

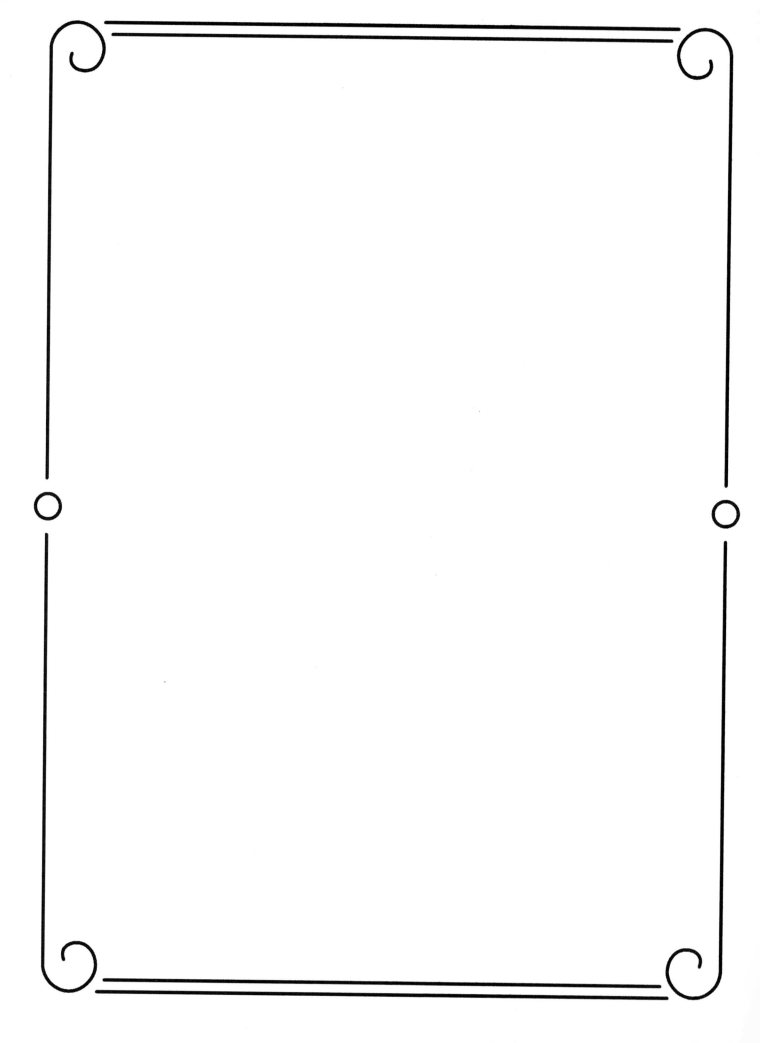

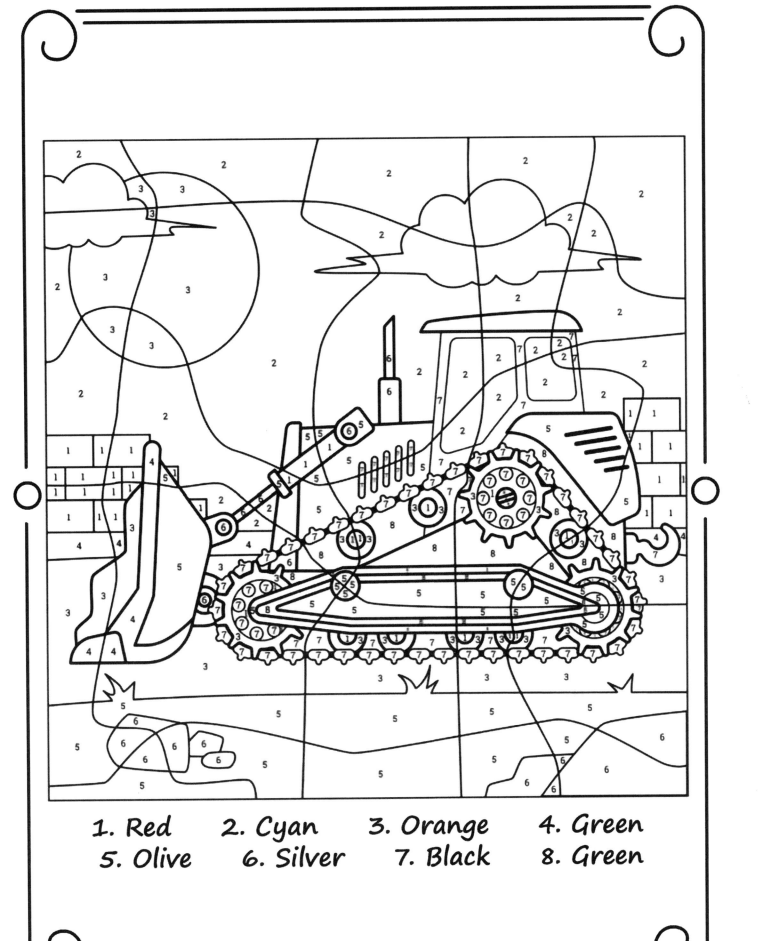

1. Red   2. Cyan   3. Orange   4. Green
5. Olive   6. Silver   7. Black   8. Green

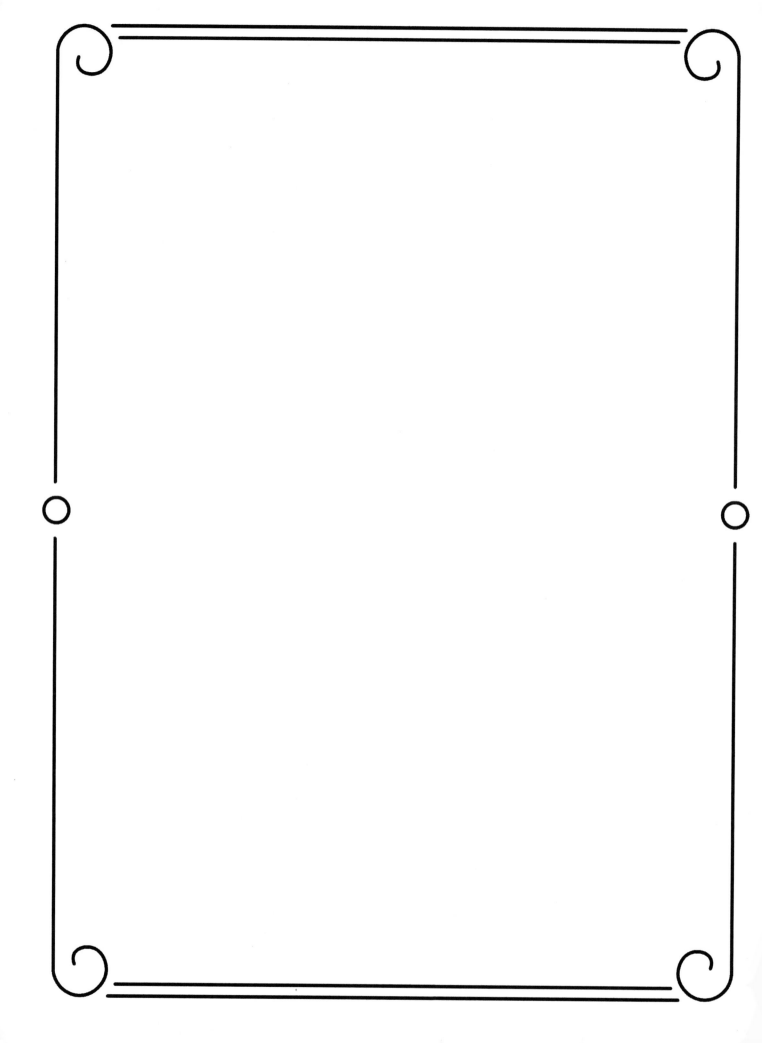

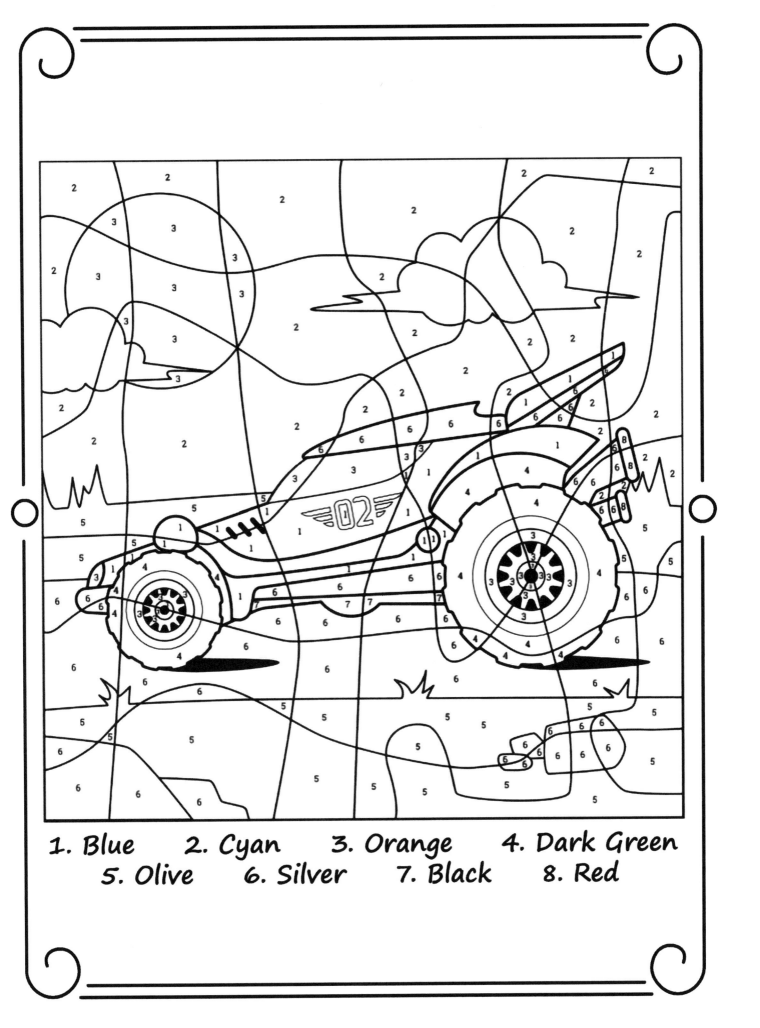

1. Blue   2. Cyan   3. Orange   4. Dark Green
5. Olive   6. Silver   7. Black   8. Red

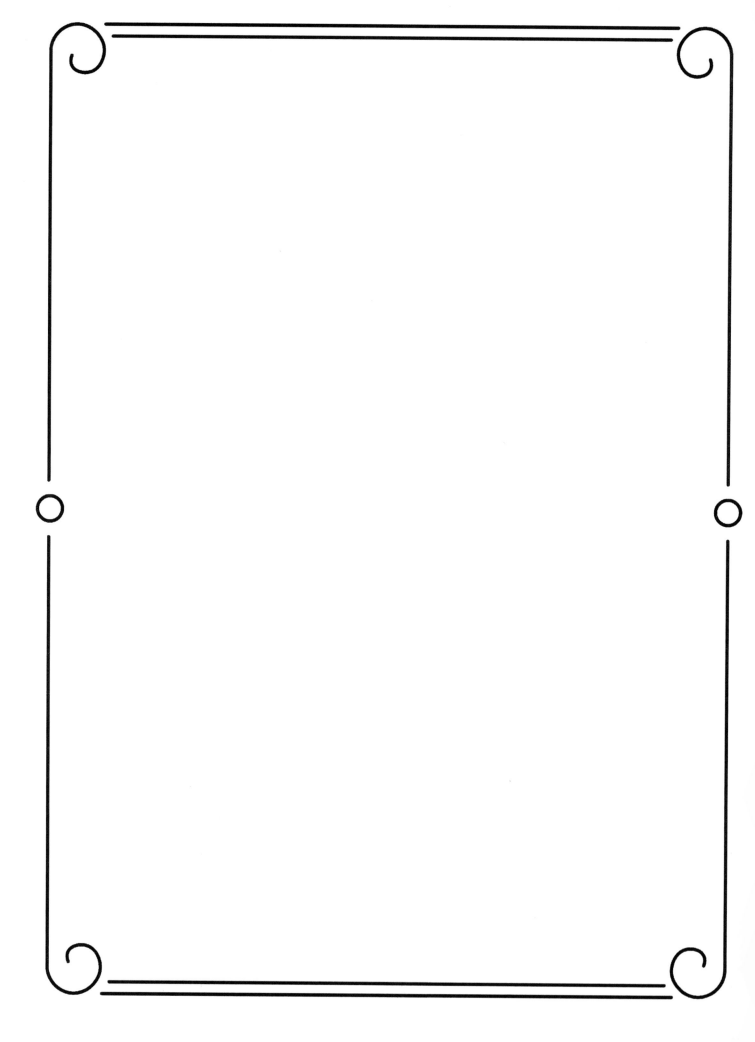

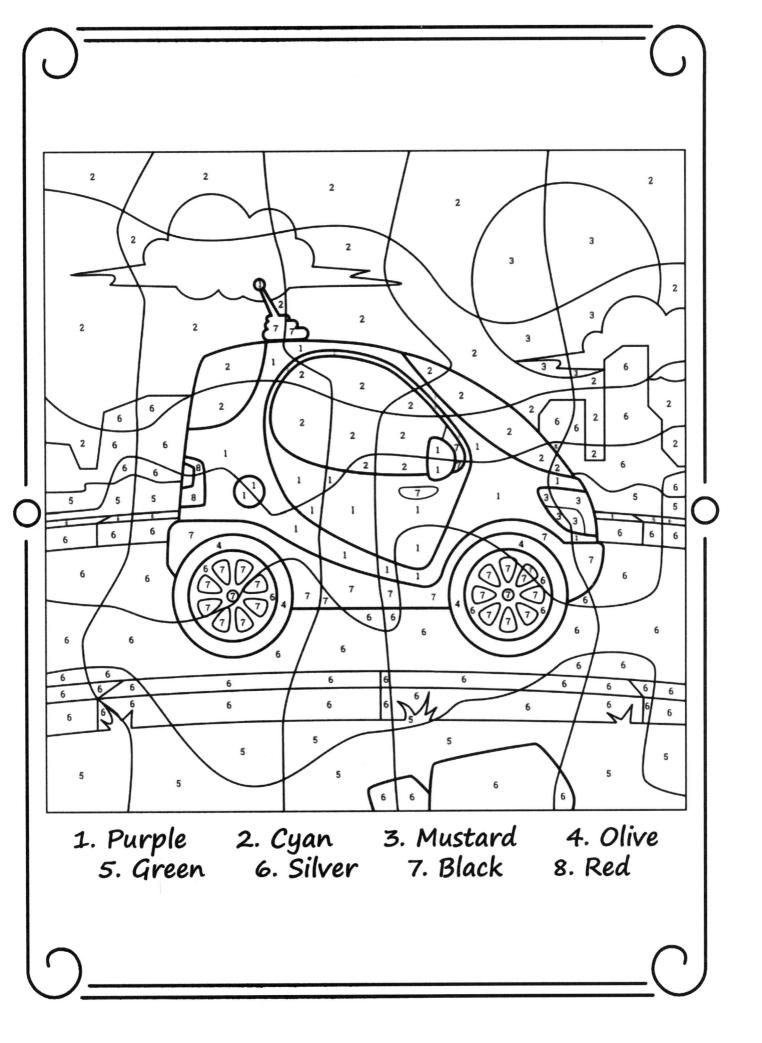

1. Purple　　2. Cyan　　3. Mustard　　4. Olive
5. Green　　6. Silver　　7. Black　　8. Red

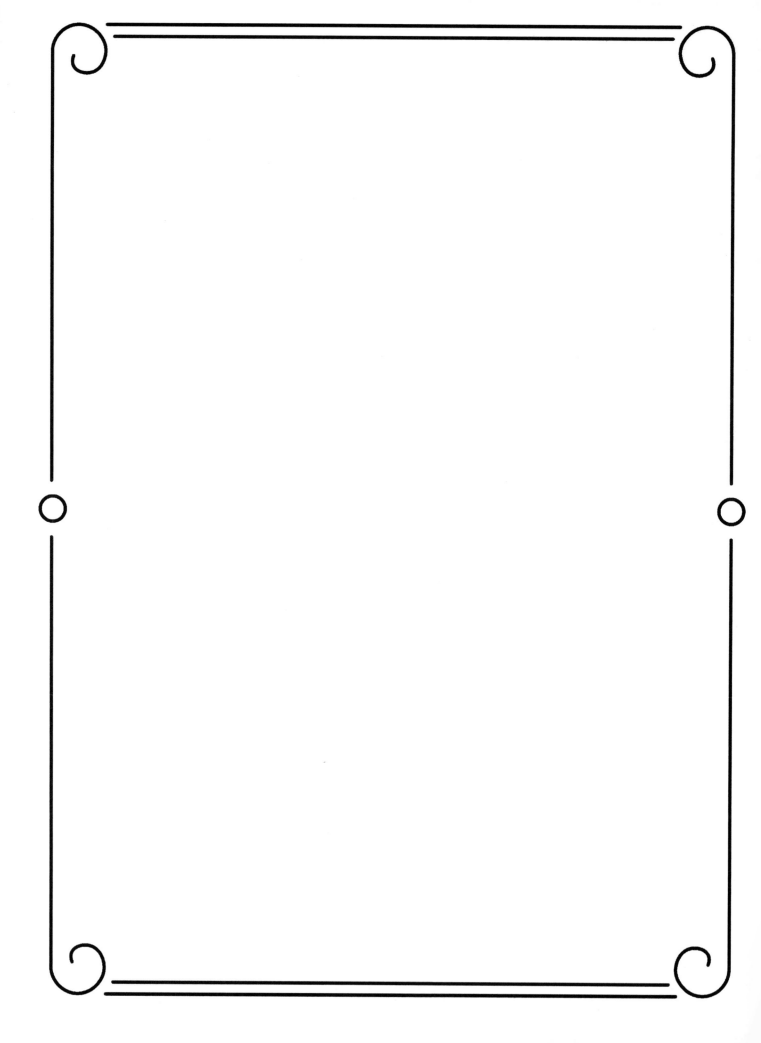

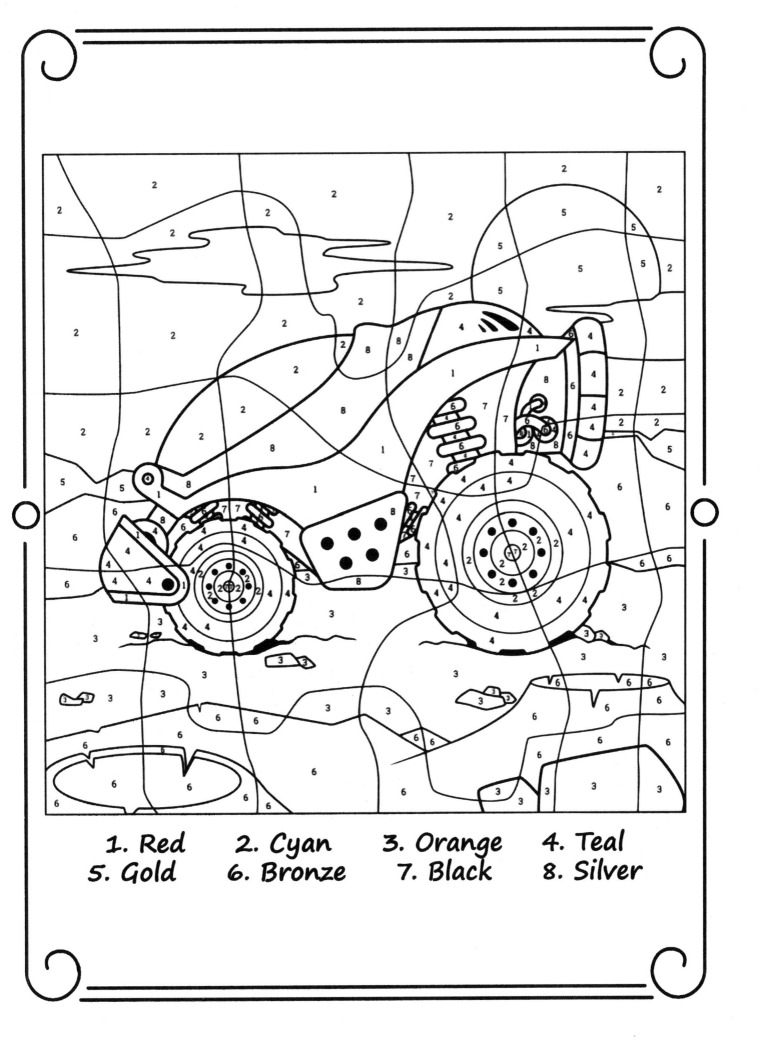

1. Red   2. Cyan   3. Orange   4. Teal
5. Gold   6. Bronze   7. Black   8. Silver

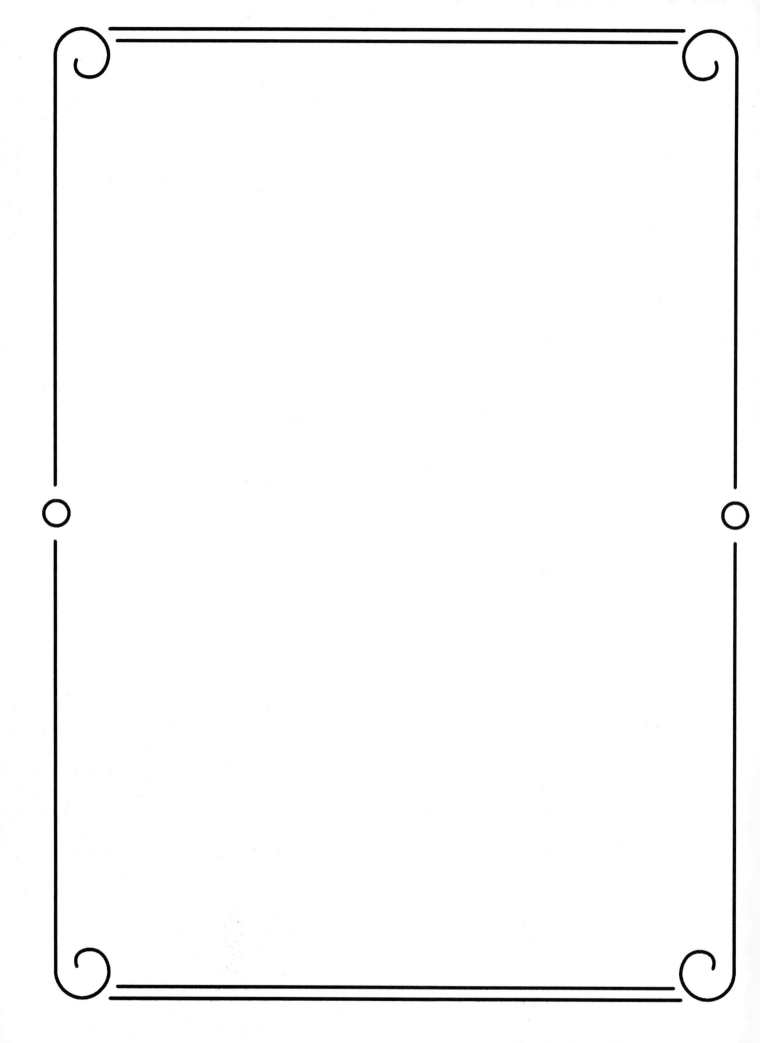

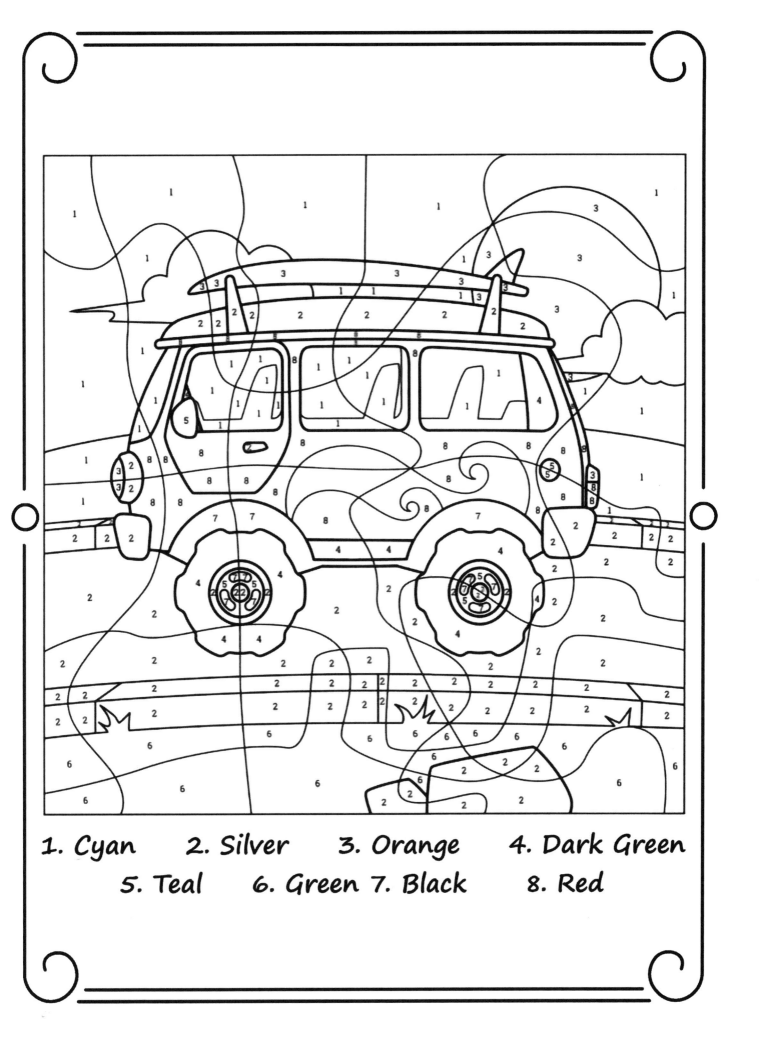

1. Cyan   2. Silver   3. Orange   4. Dark Green
5. Teal   6. Green 7. Black   8. Red

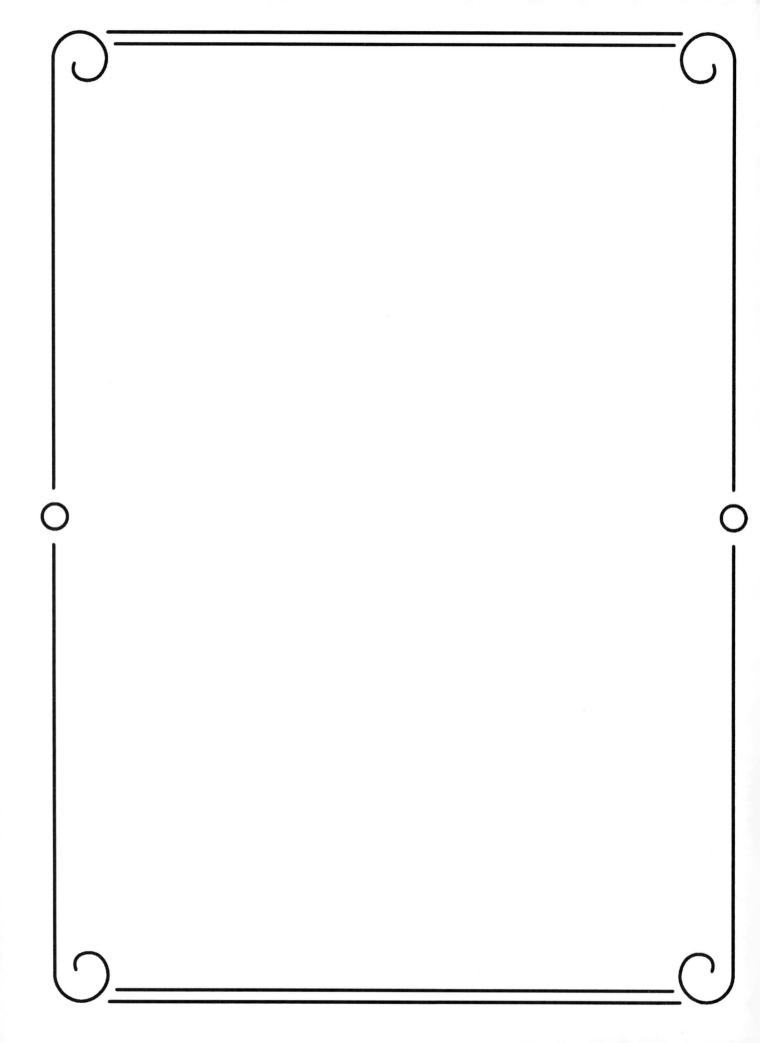

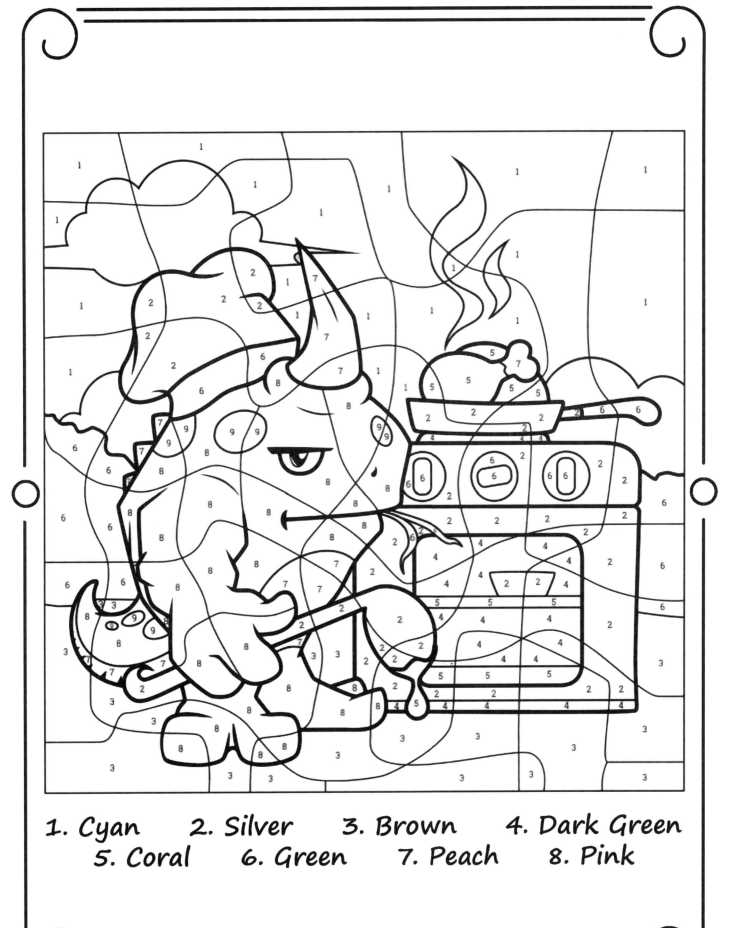

1. Cyan   2. Silver   3. Brown   4. Dark Green
5. Coral   6. Green   7. Peach   8. Pink

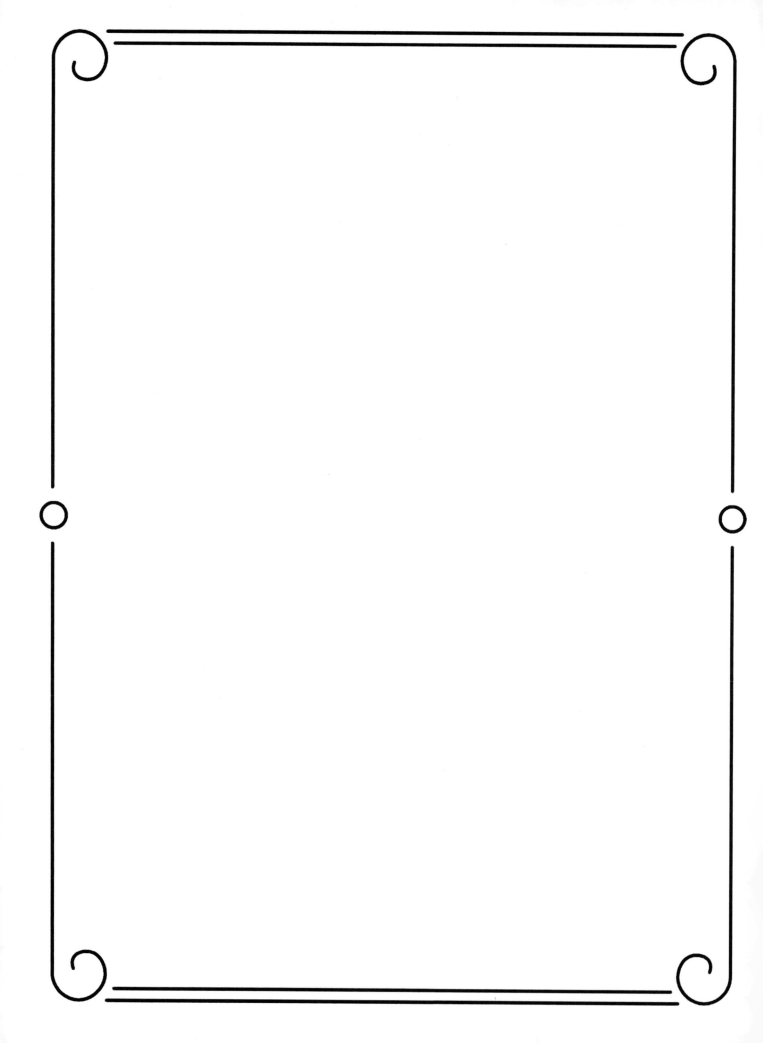

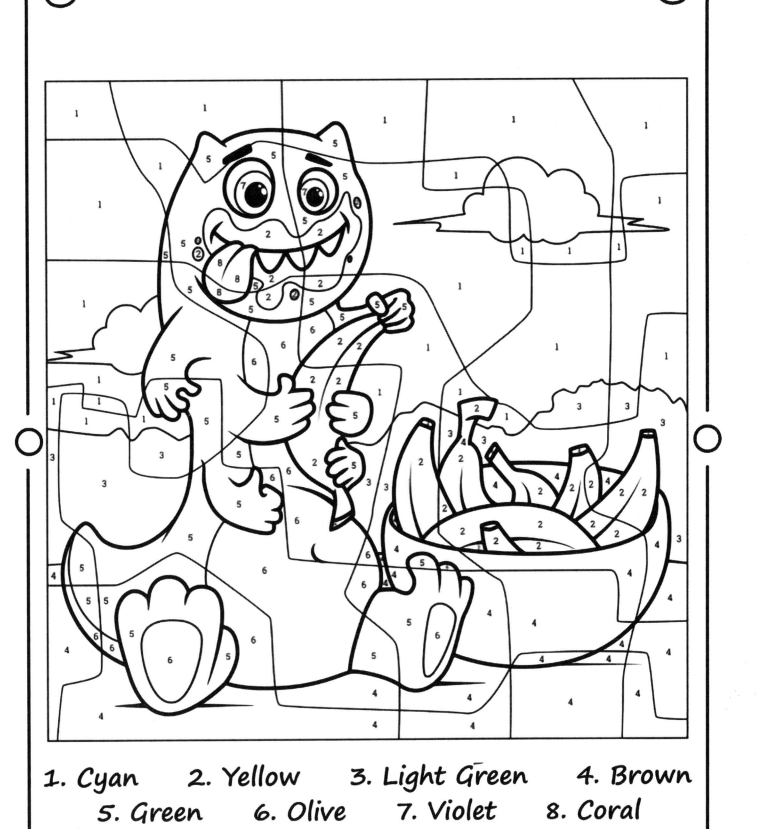

1. Cyan   2. Yellow   3. Light Green   4. Brown
5. Green   6. Olive   7. Violet   8. Coral

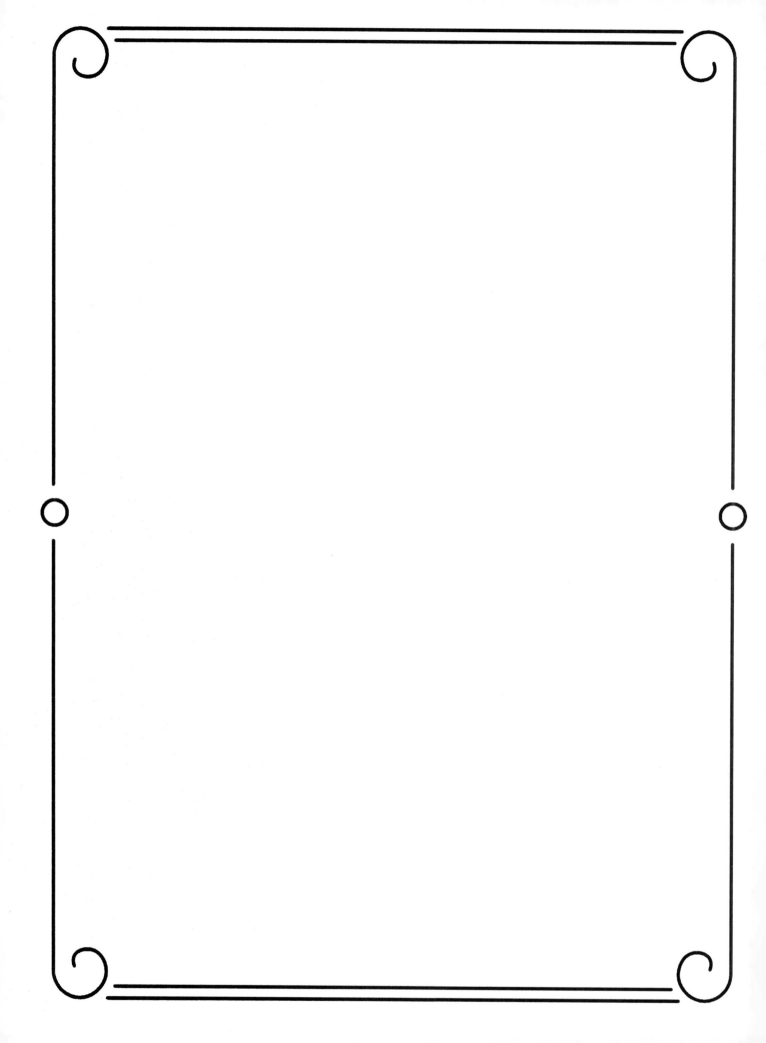

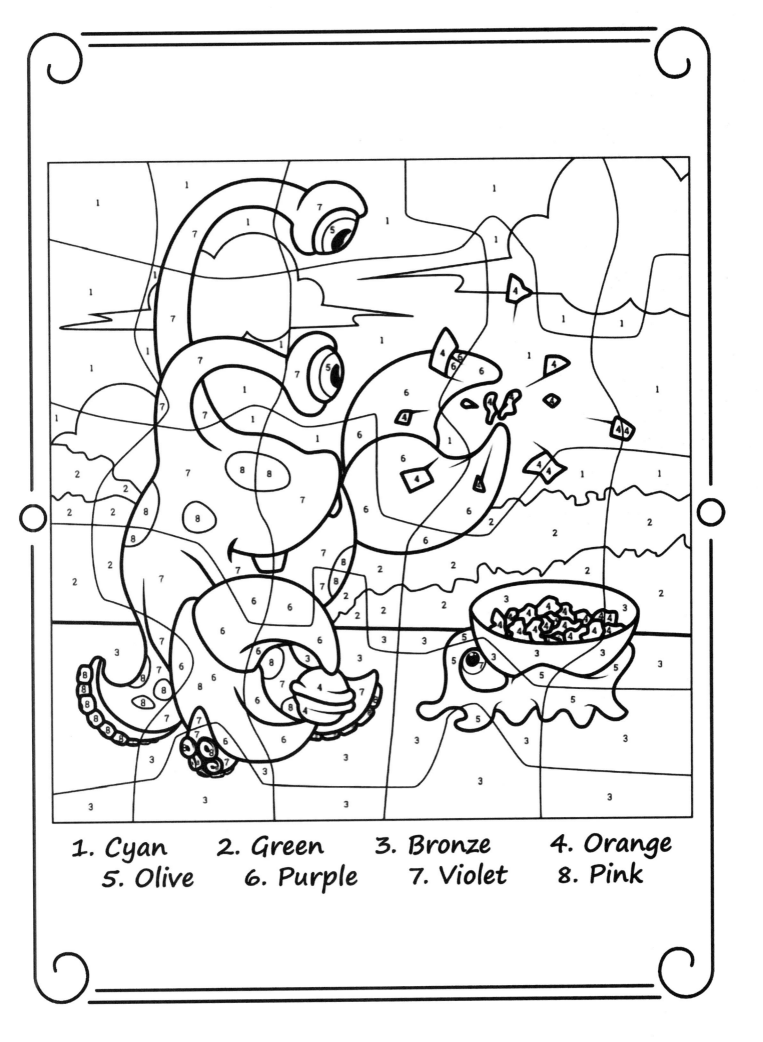

1. Cyan   2. Green   3. Bronze   4. Orange
5. Olive   6. Purple   7. Violet   8. Pink

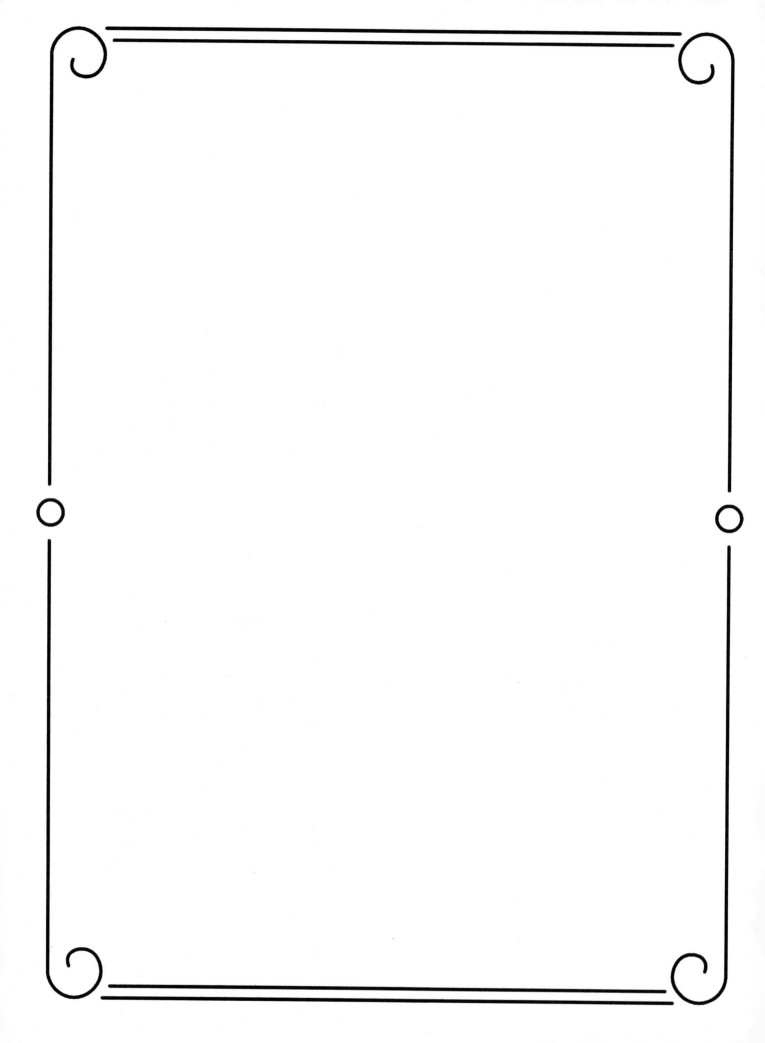

1. Cyan   2. Yellow   3. Teal   4. Olive
5. Green   6. Red   7. Orange   8. Silver

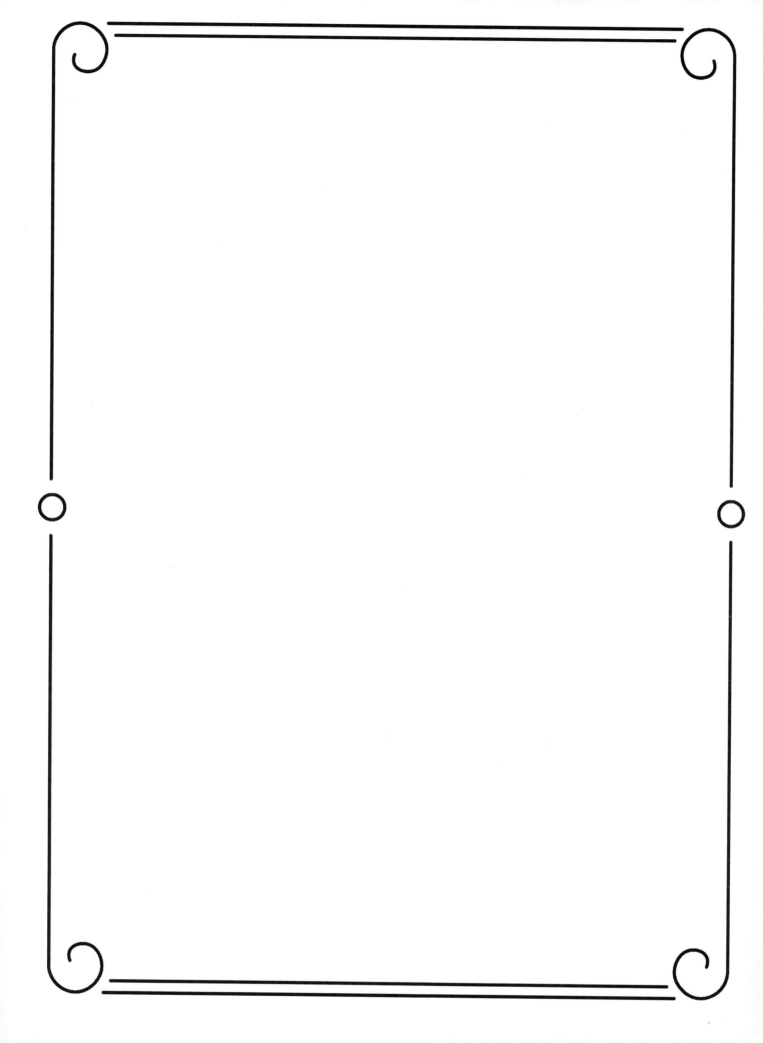

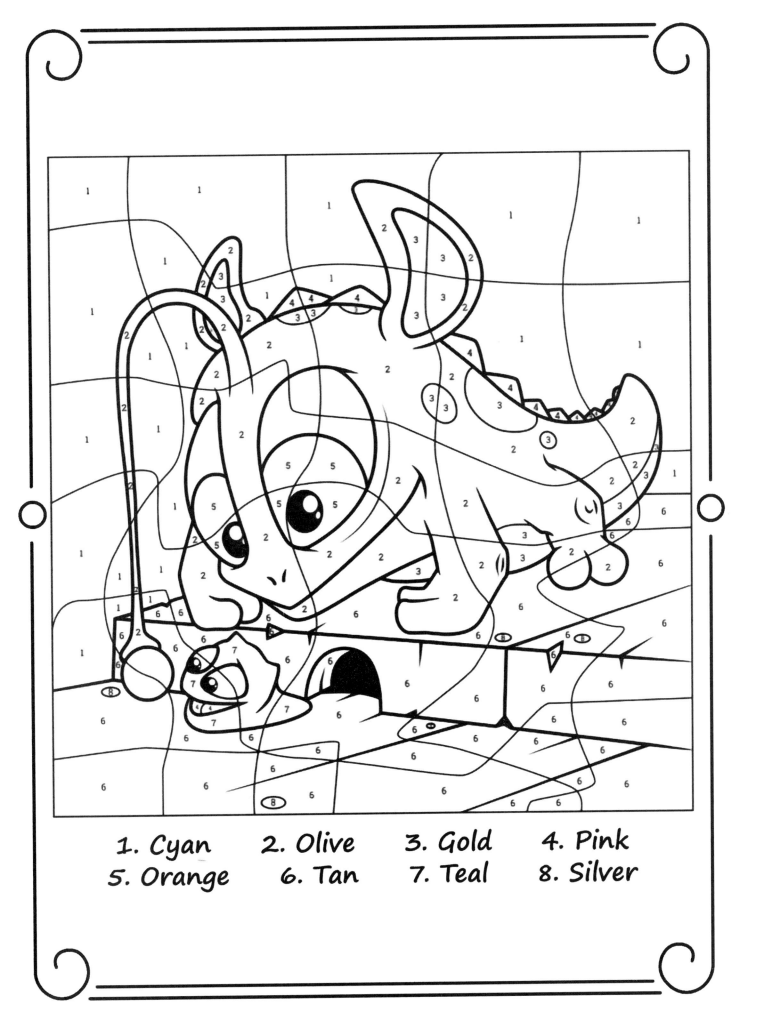

1. Cyan   2. Olive   3. Gold   4. Pink
5. Orange   6. Tan   7. Teal   8. Silver

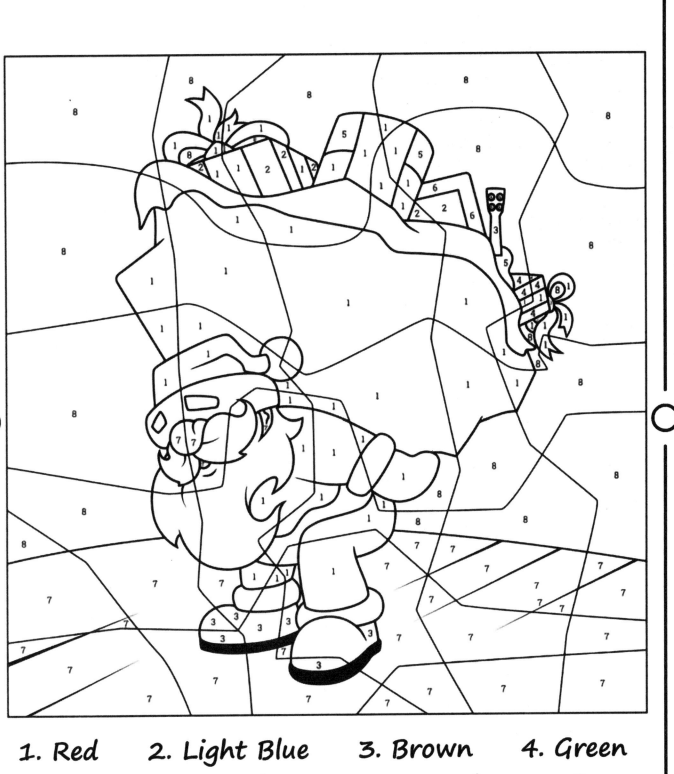

1. Red   2. Light Blue   3. Brown   4. Green
5. Orange   6. Dark Green   7. Peach   8. Cyan

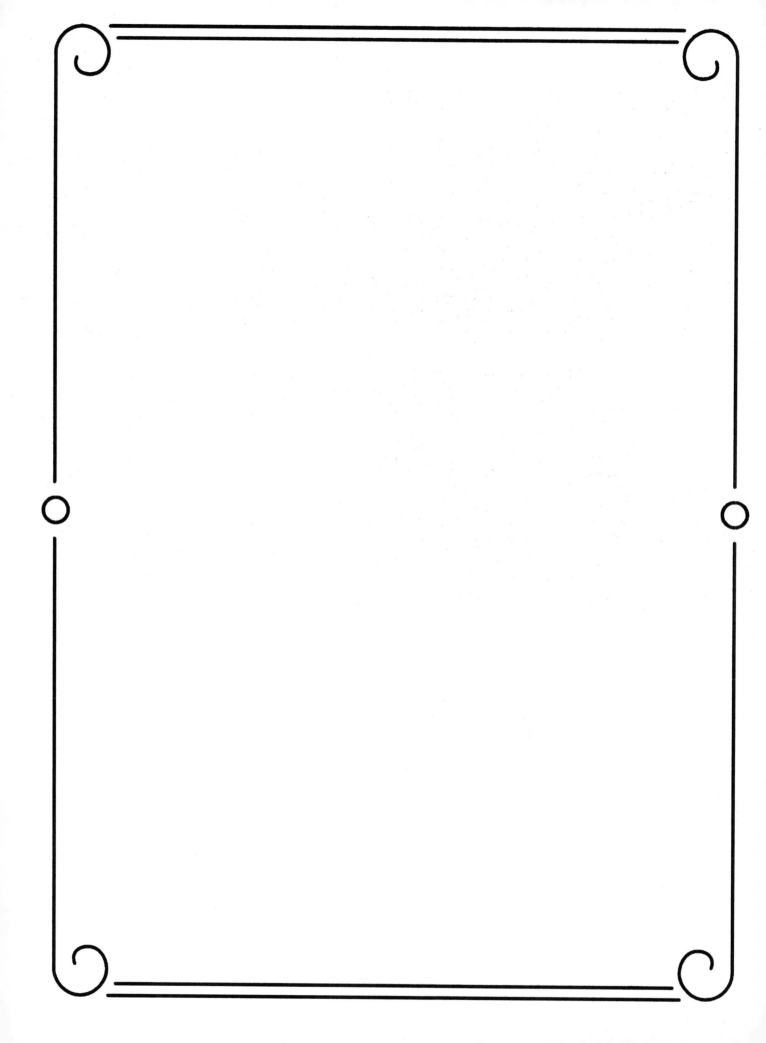

1. Red   2. Charcoal   3. Orange   4. Peach

5. Navy Blue   6. Mustard   7. Black   8. Mauve

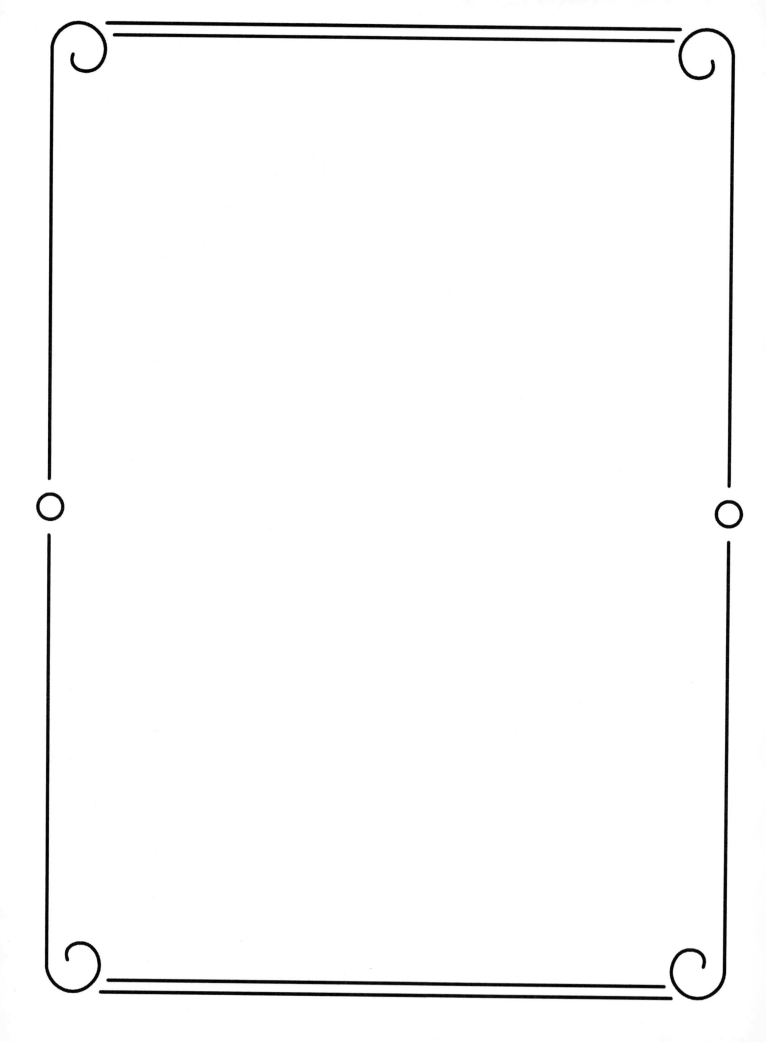

1. Green   2. Orange   3. Purple

4. Lime   5. Cyan

Dark Green=1 Gold=2 Chocolate=3 Pink=4
Brown=5 Orange=6 Light Blue=7 Blue=8

1 -grey   2 -brown   3 -green   4 -yellow
5 -blue   6 -purple

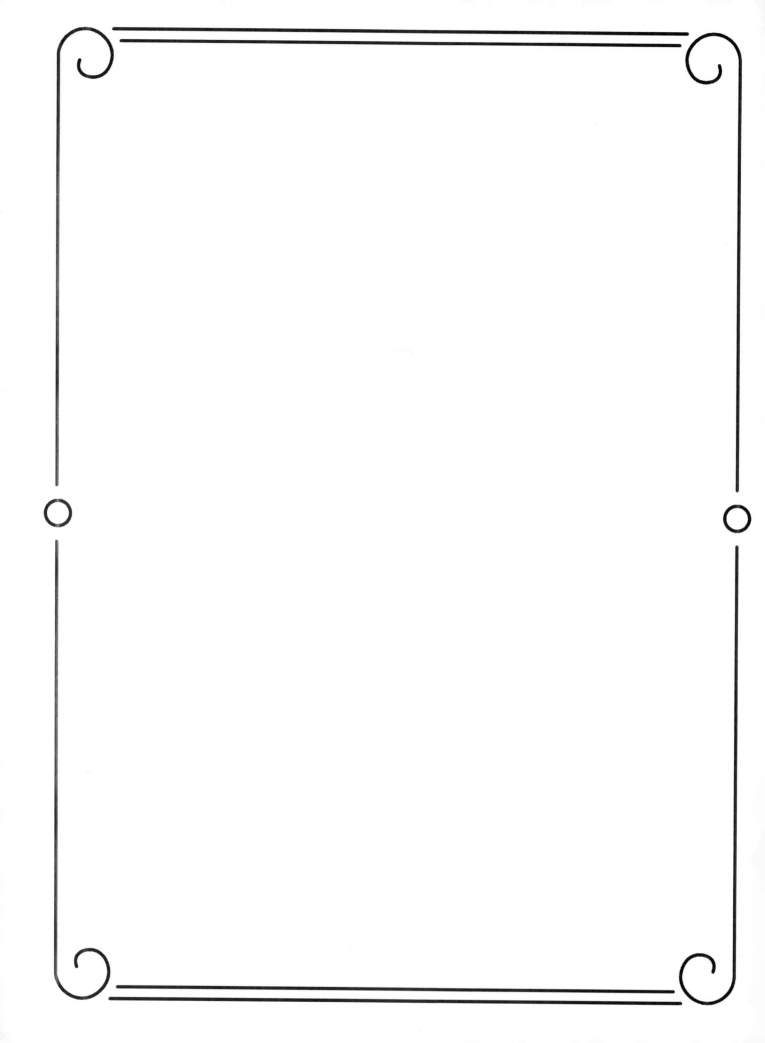

1 -black   2 -red   3 -pink   4 -cream
5 -white   6 -purple

1 -dark brown   2 -light brown   3 -brown   4 -dark pink
5 -light blue   6 -blue   7 -dark yellow   8 -navy blue

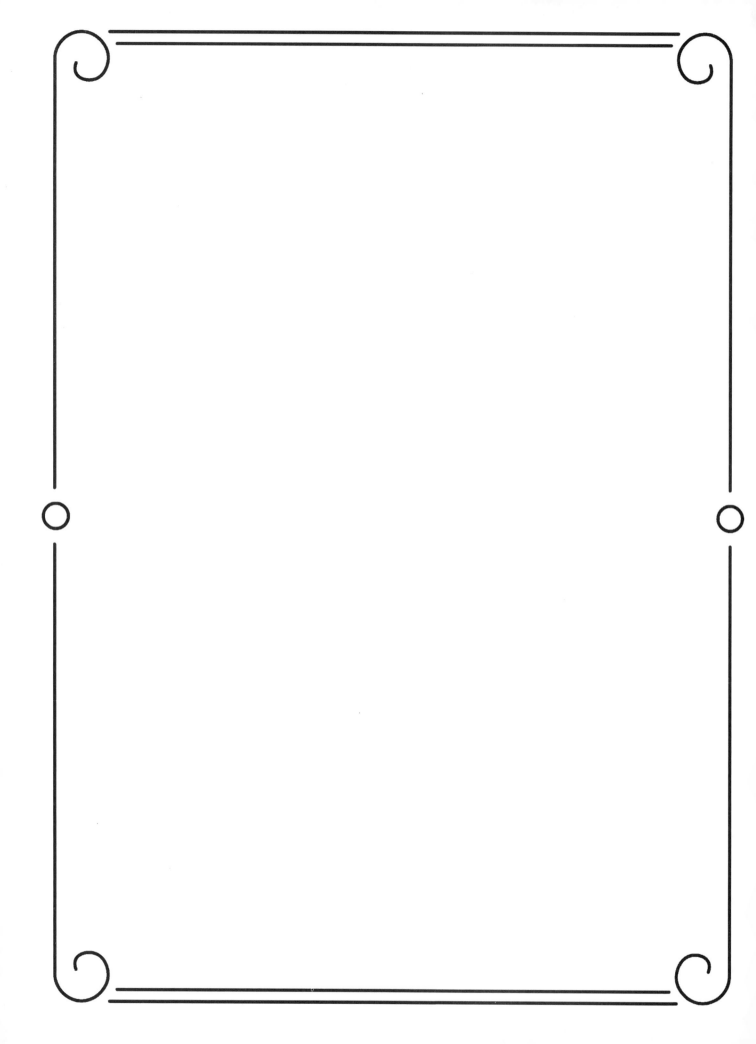

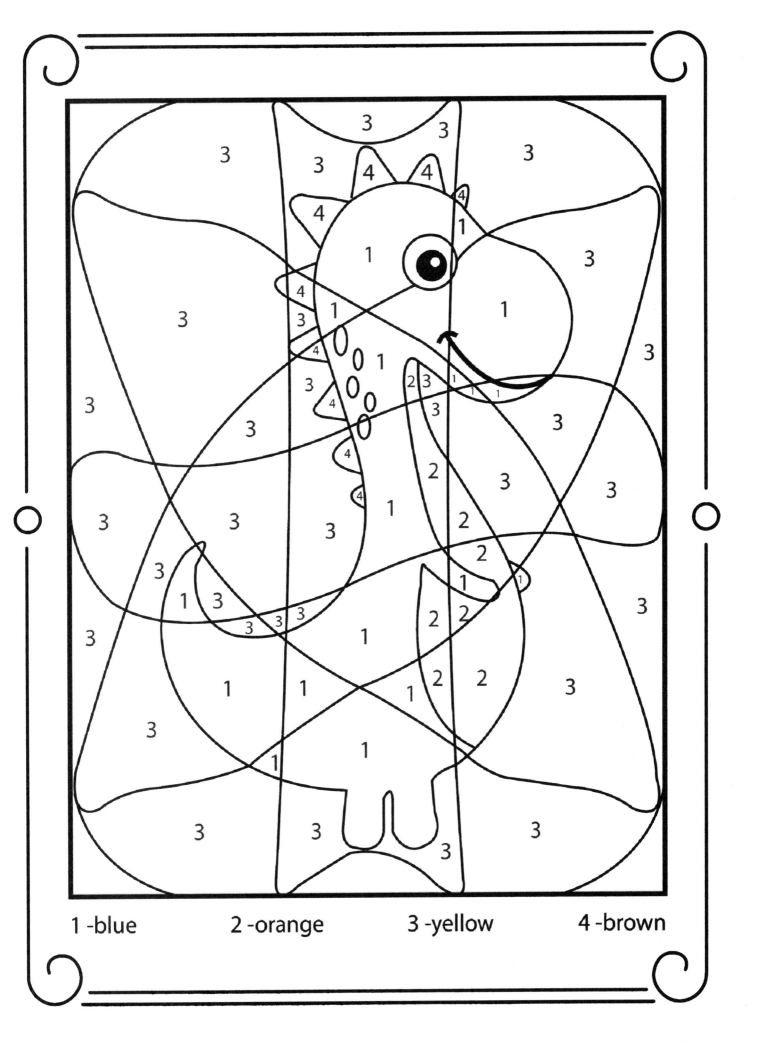

1 -blue   2 -orange   3 -yellow   4 -brown

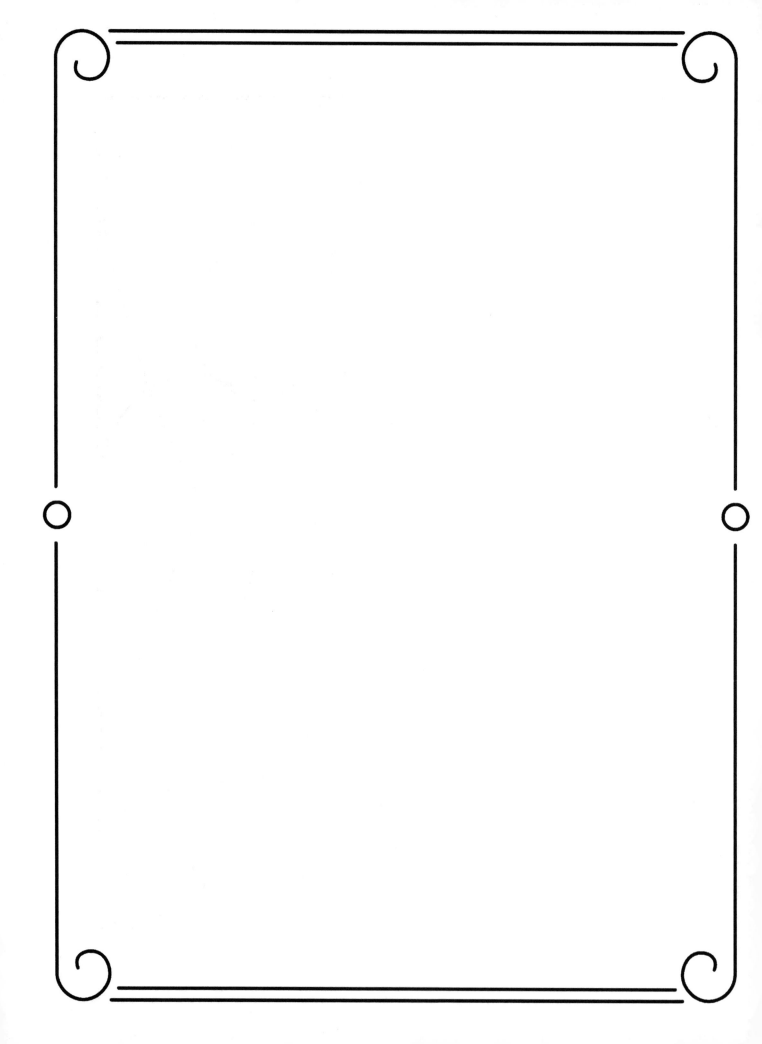

1 -navy blue　　2 -light blue　　3 -dark blue　　4 -brown

5 -light brown　　6 -blue　　7 -pink　　8 -light green

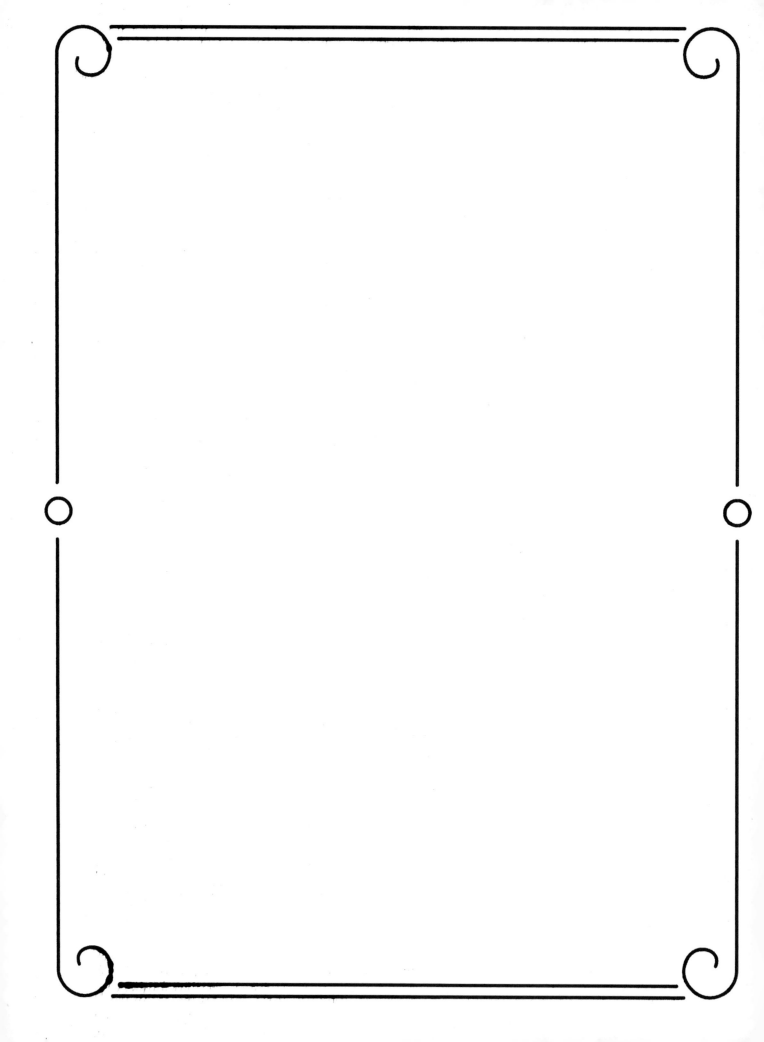

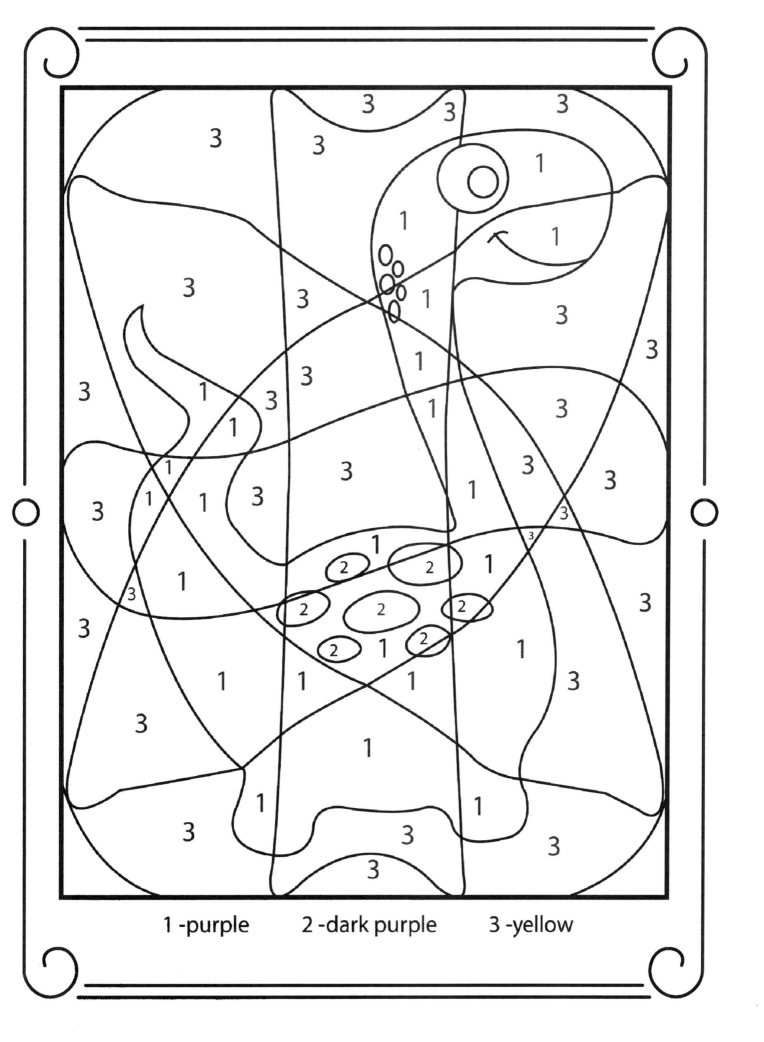

1 -purple   2 -dark purple   3 -yellow

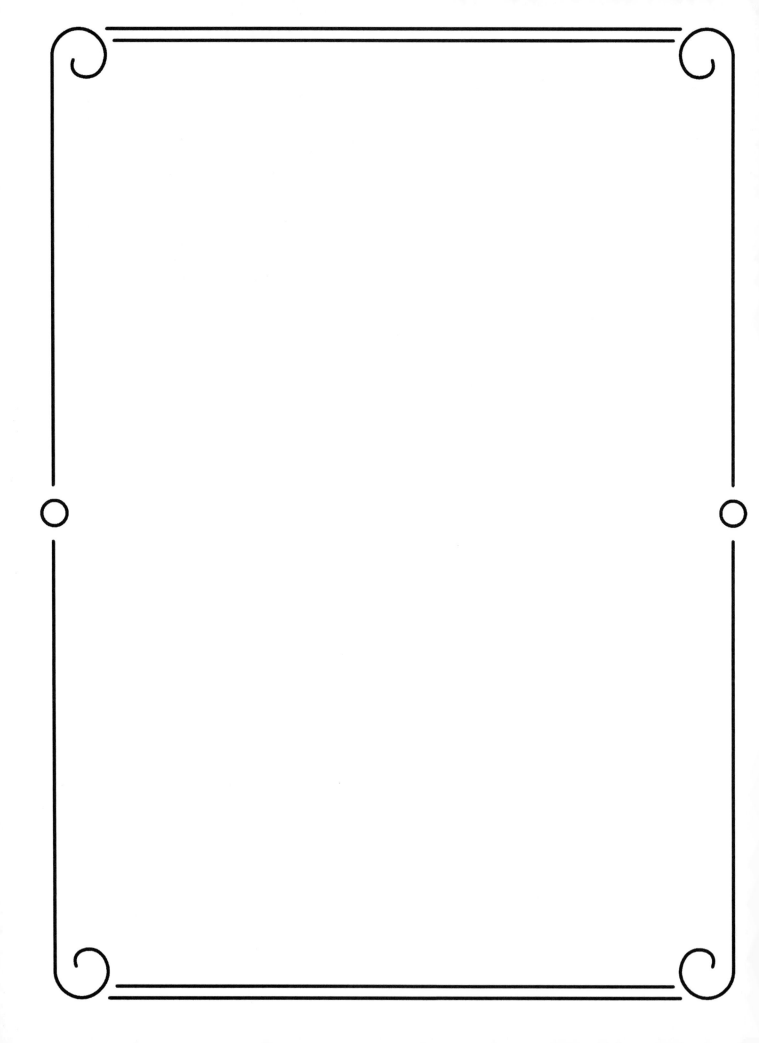

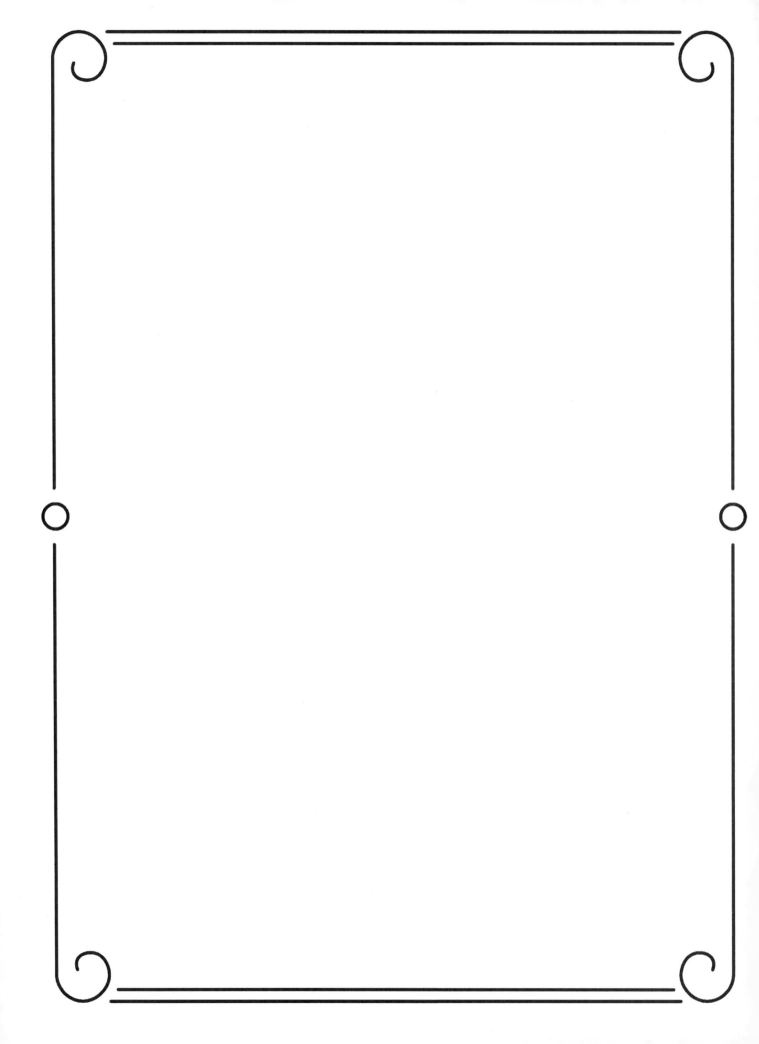

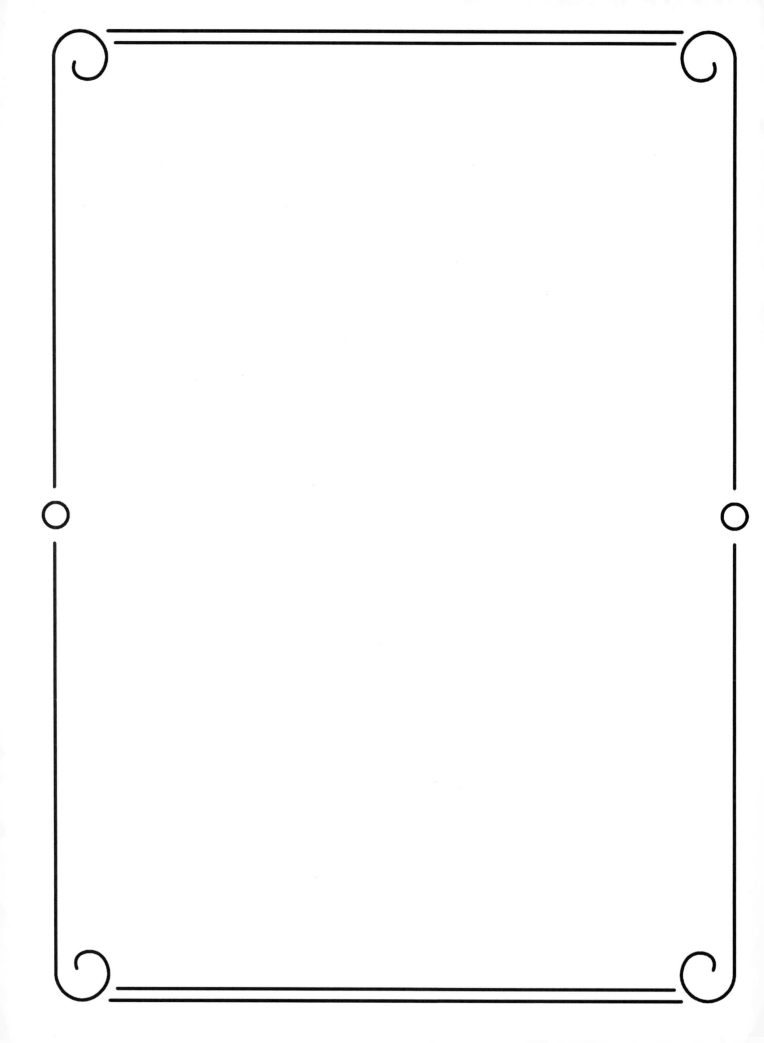

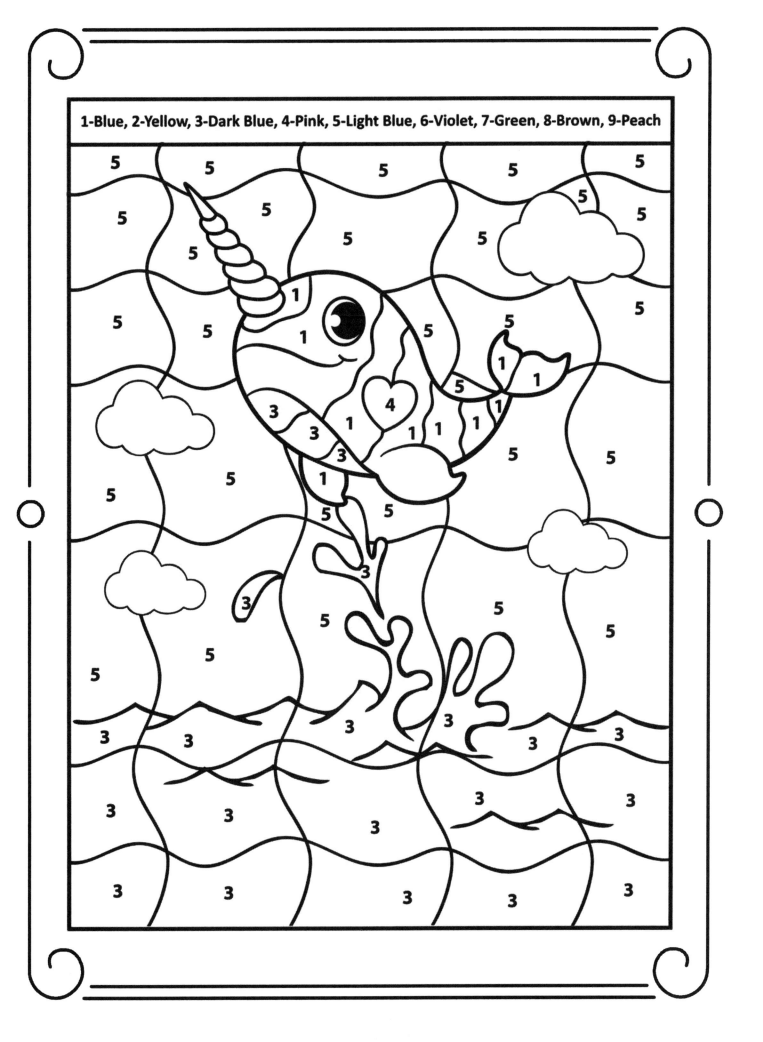

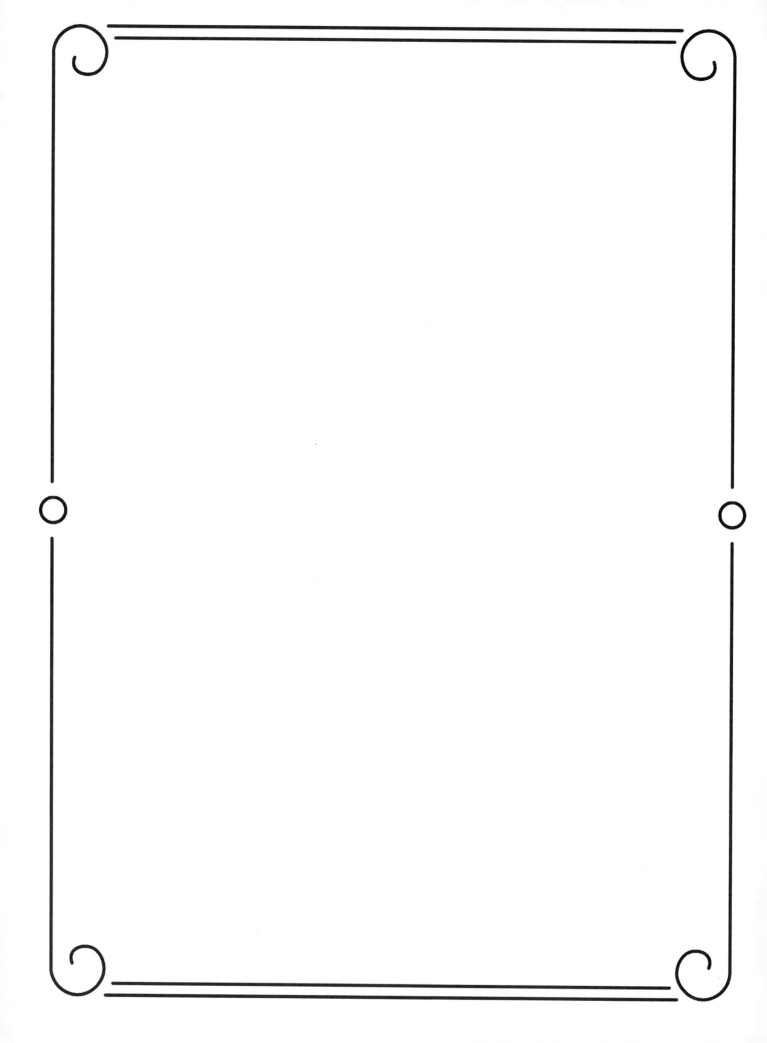

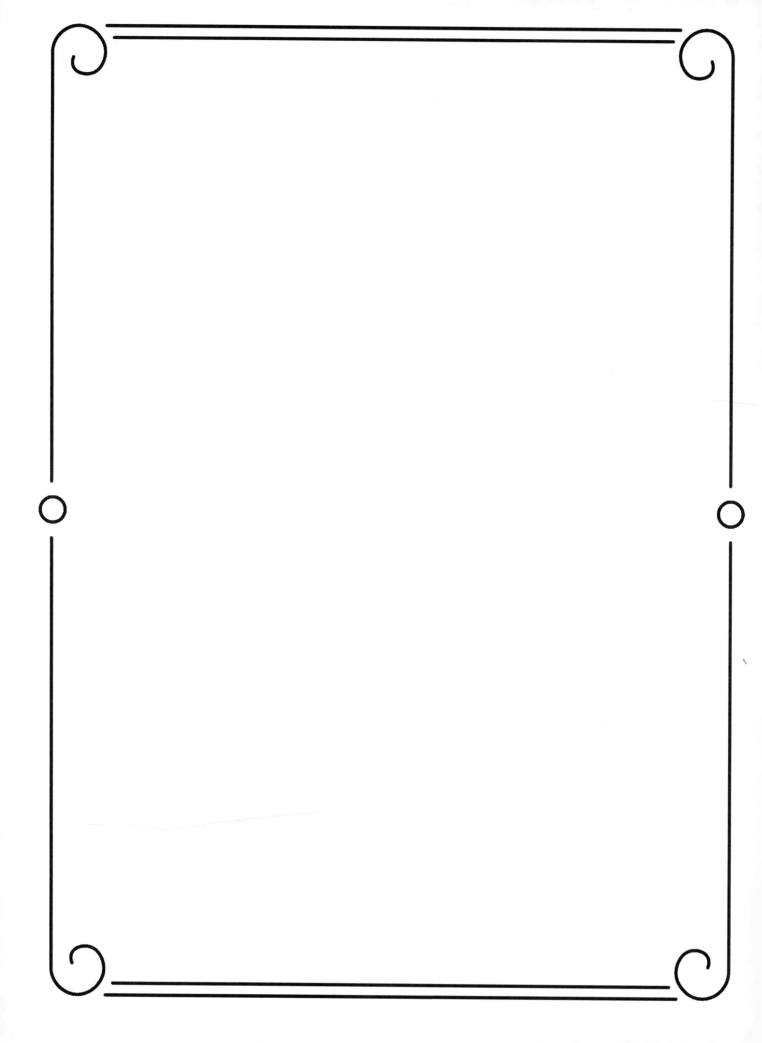

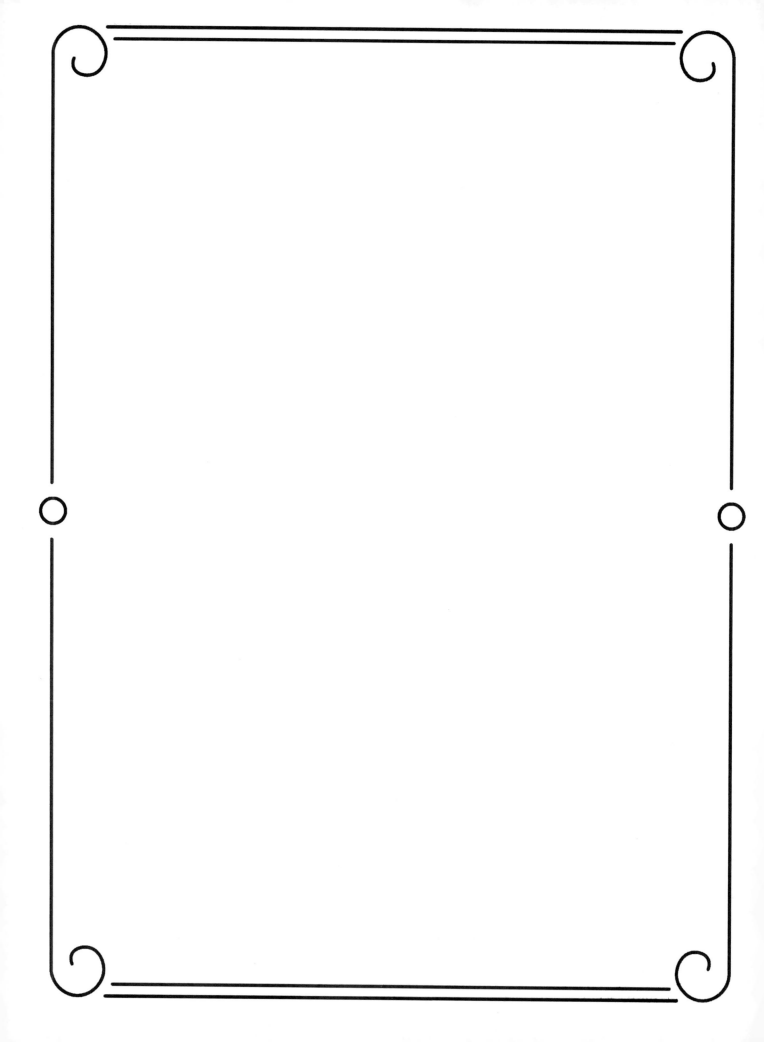

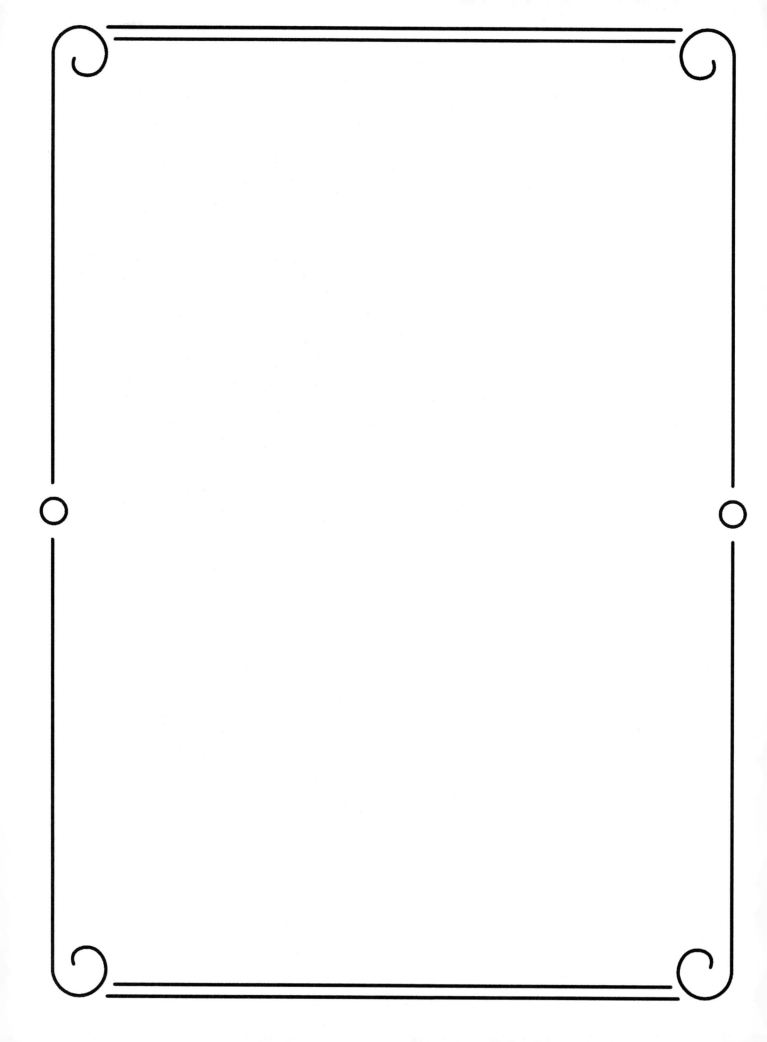